High Flyers

To Hester and David
To Rachel, Beth, Laura, Sarah and Scott
To all those chief executives who gave up their time to talk to us

HIGH FLYERS
An Anatomy of Managerial Success

Charles J. Cox
and
Cary L. Cooper

Basil Blackwell

Copyright © Charles J. Cox and Cary L. Cooper 1988

First published 1988

Basil Blackwell Ltd
108 Cowley Road, Oxford, OX4 1JF, UK

Basil Blackwell Inc.
432 Park Avenue South, Suite 1503
New York, NY 10016, USA

All rights reserved. Except for the quotation of short passages for the purposes of criticism and review, no part of this publication may be reproduced, stored in a retrieval system, or transmitted, in any form or by any means, electronic, mechanical, photocopying, recording or otherwise, without the prior permission of the publisher.

Except in the United States of America, this book is sold subject to the condition that it shall not, by way of trade or otherwise, be lent, re-sold, hired out, or otherwise circulated without the publisher's prior consent in any form of binding or cover other than that in which it is published and without a similar condition including this condition being imposed on the subsequent purchaser.

British Library Cataloguing in Publication Data
Cox, Charles
 High flyers : an anatomy of managerial success.
 1. Business firms. Executives. Success
 I. Title II. Cooper, Cary L. (Cary Lynn),
 1940–
 658.4'09
 ISBN 0–631–14066–2

Library of Congress Cataloging in Publication Data
Cox, Charles.
 High flyers.

 Bibliography: p.
 Includes index.
 1. Success in business. I. Cooper, Cary L.
 II. Title.
 HF5386.C875 1988   658.4'09   88–5070
 ISBN 0–631–14066–2

Typeset in 11 on 13pt Bembo
by Photo-graphics, Honiton, Devon.
Printed in Great Britain by
T.J. Press, Padstow

Contents

1 The High Flyers: Introduction — 1

2 Origins, Childhood and Education — 8

3 Career Development — 23

4 Work and Motivation — 47

5 Values — 70

6 Managerial Skills — 86

7 Management Philosophy — 106

8 Personality — 126

9 The Anatomy of Managerial Success — 156

References — 177

Index — 184

1
THE HIGH FLYERS: INTRODUCTION

There have been many studies of what managers do. Some, like those of Rosemary Stewart and H. H. Mintzberg, looked at how managers spend their time and what roles they play. Others, like R. E. Boyatzis, have attempted to tease out the skills and behaviours shown by successful managers. Recently, there have also been a number of biographical studies of leading managers, mainly those with considerable entrepreneurial flair, for example, the books by Elizabeth Hennessy, Carol Kennedy and Robert Bruce. These, by and large, document individuals' careers, and tell us about the decisions they made and the deals they did, but tell us nothing about the person themselves. Another recent approach has been to look at the characteristics of successful organizations, as was done by Peters and Waterman in the USA and Goldsmith and Clutterbuck in the UK. Again, only by inference can one get to the characteristics of the successful manager.

Cooper and Hingley's study of *The Change Makers* does give insight into the individual, but, while the majority of the people included are managers, they again tend to be of the 'famous entrepreneur' variety. Other books that have concentrated more on the characteristics of the successful individual are Leah Hertz's study of women who run their own businesses, *The Business Amazons*, which again tends to the entrepreneurial, and G. Copeman's comparative study of chief executives in the United States, Britain and Germany, which has chapters on skills, motivation, required qualities and business philosophy. Our book is intended to develop these aspects of the study of management. It is an attempt to gain greater insight into the characteristics, not of the entrepreneur, but of the successful manager working *within* the organization.

Who are the Successful Managers?

Any discussion of successful managers raises the question of defining 'success'. For the purposes of this study, we have avoided the tricky philosophical issues by defining the *successful manager* as one who reaches the top of a major organization. As many of our interviewees rather modestly pointed out, the fact that they had reached the position of chief executive did not necessarily mean that they were 'good' managers. However, it seems to us that it is not an unreasonable assumption that, if an individual has reached the top position in a major and successful organization, he or she is probably a pretty good manager. But, in any case, the focus of interest is success, and success in this case means reaching the top.

To obtain an appropriate sample, we selected from the Kompas Index, at random, companies of over 1000 employees and with a successful financial record. Companies were selected from the North of England, the Midlands and the London area. We then wrote to the chief executive officer or managing director, explaining the purpose of the study, and asking if he would be prepared to take part in an interview and complete some questionnaires. We wrote to sixty-four individuals in all, of whom forty-five agreed to take part. They were all male. Since no women MDs came up through our random procedure – they represent, in any case, a very small number nationally – the use of the pronoun 'he', from here on, is because we are dealing with a male population and not from incipient chauvinism!

Introduction

The final sample included two MDs whose organizations do not strictly conform to the criterion of being above 1000 employees. Both were included because their companies' gross sales and net profits were high, even though the number of employees was below the 1000 figure. Apart from this, the organizations ranged in size from just over a thousand to tens of thousands of employees. Most of them are well-known names, but, as confidentiality was guaranteed both to individuals and to their company, the actual organizations are not listed. A wide range of industries is represented, as shown in table 1.1.

What did we Want to Know about MDs?

The interviews, in general, took between an hour and an hour and a half. A few went on longer, perhaps to two hours. The

Table 1.1 Distribution of companies by industry

Industry	No. of companies
Engineering	13
Electrical	2
Food	3
Finance	2
Public utility	1
Packaging	1
Toiletries	1
Printing	1
Textile and clothing	5
Civil engineering and contracting	4
Safety products	1
Chemicals	4
Pharmaceuticals	4
Conglomerates	2
Paper	1
Total	45

purpose, as stated above, was to gain insight into the characteristics of the successful manager. The areas covered were therefore selected as those most likely to throw light on what *makes* a successful person, as suggested by previous research and our implicit theories of managerial behaviour. The background to each area will be discussed more fully in the appropriate chapter, but, briefly, they were as follows.

Family background   There is a very large literature on the effects of childhood events, and parental and sibling relationships, on later life. We therefore wanted to see if we could detect anything in the early life of our managers to account for their later success, focusing particularly on *parental relationships* and *significant childhood events*.

Education   Is there anything distinctive about their educational background? Could we detect any trends that seemed to be significant? To help answer these questions, we collected data on our managers' *schools, universities* and *other education*.

Career pattern   Do successful managers rise rapidly and meteorically or slowly and steadily? Information was gathered on *job changes* and *rate of progression*. We were also interested in the part played by formal *management-development programmes* in their careers, and the *role of mentors*, if any.

Orientation to work   We were particularly interested in their *work pattern*, how hard they worked and what *motivated* them. What *skills* did they require? What was their *management philosophy*?

Philosophy of life   What is their orientation to life outside work? What are their 'life values'? What do they do in their spare time? We collected data on their *recreational activities, family* and *values*.

The interview itself was semi-structured, the interviewer broaching a topic with open-ended questions and encouraging

Introduction

the MD to talk. A checklist was used to ensure that all topics were covered. Most interviews were recorded, but half a dozen chief executives were unwilling to have their comments tape-recorded. Respondents were asked directly about areas such as motivation and values, but were also asked questions like 'What advice would you give to a son or daughter about being successful?' and 'What would you like to see as your epitaph?', in the hope that more underlying assumptions about values could be teased out. Interestingly, many managers had difficulty with the second question, possibly because of the difficulty of dealing with the implication of their own mortality.

In addition to the interview, we used a number of questionnaires, beginning with the 16PF Personality Inventory (see Cattell's *The Scientific Analysis of Personality*), which measures sixteen personality characteristics (see chapter 8). A questionnaire to measure type A/B behaviour patterns was also implemented. Friedman and Rosenman (in Rosenman, Friedman and Strauss, 'CHD in the Western collaborative group study') identified a set of behavioural characteristics in individuals prone to coronary heart disease, which they labelled type A behaviour. The pattern includes such behaviours as striving for achievement, competitiveness, impatience, a sense of urgency and over-commitment to work. Type B stresses the opposites. The popular stereotype of the big-business executive includes many type A characteristics, so it seemed desirable to investigate this widely held belief.

We also used the Kirton Adaptation–Innovation Inventory, which is a measure concerned with creativity and coping with change. Briefly, *adaptors* tend to originate change only within the existing system, while *innovators* will challenge and modify the system. Kirton has indicated that there are important implications for 'adaptors' and 'innovators' working together in an organization, and we were interested to see which orientation was shown by those who reach the top. Finally, respondents were asked to complete the Leadership Opinion Questionnaire. This is based on the work of E. A. Fleishman and indicates whether the manager, in his dealings with subordinates, is oriented towards *consideration*, reflecting mutual trust, warmth and respect, or *structure*, which emphasizes control and goal orientation. It is possible to gain a high or low score on either or both dimensions. The results from the questionnaires will be discussed in the appropriate chapters.

Why do we Want to Know about Successful Top Managers?

The chief executive and his team are one of the most important influences on the culture of an organization, and thus on both its ultimate success and the wellbeing of its members, and yet we know very little of the characteristics of successful people at this level. There are many theories and beliefs but very few data. As M. Sorcher says in *Predicting Executive Success*:

> While the senior executives who select chiefs generally agree on a number of characteristics and abilities they believe are predictive, very few of them express the same confidence and the same characteristics and abilities. For example, some say vision is the most important, others say that motivating a team is paramount, and some predict success mostly from analytical ability. They will agree, when asked, that the other qualities are also important – but they do not typically look for those qualities or abilities on their own initiative.

Our own experience confirms this view. We approached a number of eminent chairmen and chief executives of major organizations not included in the sample we interviewed, and asked for their views on the required characteristics of top managers. There was, as Sorcher indicates, considerable overlap in their views, but also some important differences on both content and emphasis. Samples of these views are quoted at appropriate places in the text. Our hope is that in this book we can define the characteristics of those successful individuals who have made it to the top of major companies, in a way that will be helpful both for improving selection and for the development of future top executives.

Introduction

Neils Bohr is credited with the proposition that a scientist can say everything about a drop of water except that it is wet. I am sure that you will add usefully to the considerable body of literature which already exists on what constitutes a successful manager. I am not sure that I can. Successful managers come in many shapes and styles. The businesses which they run vary in organization and in products. They probably all share a certain appetite for work and for success. But, particularly in the service industries, the successful chairman or chief executive officer must above all understand people and be able to motivate and manage them. It is the job of the professor of management science to define success in business; it is a CEO's job to recognize it. He need not necessarily be able to describe the winners, but he must be able to pick them

(Lord King of Wartneby, Chief Executive, British Airways)

2
ORIGINS, CHILDHOOD AND EDUCATION

The importance of childhood events in influencing adult behaviour has long been recognized in philosophical and psychological literature. Plato (428–348 BC) stated in *The Republic*: 'The first step, as you know, is always what matters most, particularly when we are dealing with those who are young and tender. That is the time when they are taking shape and when any impression we choose to make leaves a permanent mark.' This is a theme which recurs in the writings of philosophers from Plato's time until the present, but it is probably the work of Sigmund Freud which has done most to propagate this view. As he observed in *An Outline of Psychoanalysis*, 'analytic experience has convinced us of the complete truth of the common assertion that the child is psychologically father of the man and that the events of his first years are of paramount importance for his whole subsequent life.'

A common theme of much of the literature is the effects of deprivation in childhood, particularly the loss of one or both parents. There seems to be an assumption that the overcoming of early adversity contributes to later success – a form of over-compensation, perhaps. R. S. Illingworth and C. M. Illingworth in *Lessons from Childhood*, for example, assert that 'a surprisingly large number of children destined for fame lost one or both parents during childhood'. They give a list of seventy famous people who lost their parents when under the age of 10; these include Nero, Confucius, Michelangelo, Ivan the Terrible, Descartes, Newton, Robespierre, Darwin, Tolstoy, Somerset Maugham and Eichmann. It will be noted that these include, as well as the 'great and good', some of the greatest villains of history.

While these discoveries are interesting, it is dangerous, of course, to consider such studies as proving anything, since any calculations of statistical significance are impossible. The Illingworths do recognize this and give instances of famous individuals with entirely happy home backgrounds; these include Linnaeus, Jane Austen, Gandhi and Franklin Roosevelt. The reason for mentioning these studies here is that they illustrate the enduring belief that childhood does affect later life, and, indeed, it is tempting to suggest that there may well be something different about the quality of the lives of the two groups, even though both are famous. This is an area which, despite its long history, still requires further exploration.

More recent studies of managers have also looked at the significance of early events. In *The Change Makers* Cooper and Hingley, for example, found that influential managers had often experienced spearation from parents, or other trauma in childhood, giving rise to feelings of insecurity and loss. Studies by R. V. Clements (*Managers*) and Lewis and Stewart (*The Boss*) have looked at the social origins of managers, finding them to come, in general, from the higher socio-economic classes. C. B. Handy (*Understanding Organisations*) and J. Hunt (*Managing People at Work*) among others, have suggested that position in the family is important, with youngest and eldest children being more assertive than those in between. This has obvious implications for management.

Many autobiographies of successful managers also trace their adult experiences and approach to life back to particular childhood events. In *Back from the Brink*, Michael Edwardes, for example, believes his father had a strong influence on his own self-sufficiency, and to illustrate this he relates an incident when at the age of 15 he lost the outboard motor of the family boat (overboard) on a fishing trip with a friend of similar age:

My father's reaction when we rowed back to the shack was quite predictable – 'We'll leave some eggs, milk and bread for you; when you have found it phone me and I'll drive out and fetch the pair of you.' We found it after eight days of grappling and diving. The lesson was clear and simple: you make your own mistakes and you correct them yourself. No one looks after anyone from the cradle to the grave.

It is probably also significant that he regarded his father as a man who 'saw life as an obstacle course and, as part of their education, his children were required to practise on real live obstacles.' Another example is provided by H. S. Geneen in his autobiography, *Managing*, written with Alvin Moscow, in which he traces his adult optimism, enthusiasm and 'attitude towards work as a creative experience' to his father's influence and events in early childhood, which was rather lonely and had the effect of developing self-sufficiency.

There seems, then, good reason why it would be fruitful to ask our sample about their childhood and early experience.

SOCIAL ORIGINS

R. V. Clements, in *Managers*, a study of all managers in twenty-eight firms in the North-West of England, found social class to be significant: 'A comparison between the social origins of the managers in the sample, and those of the general male population, suggests that the chances of young men of higher social origins successfully becoming industrial managers have been considerably greater than those of lower social origins.' This is supported by D. Norburn, who, in a comparison of British and American corporate leaders, found that:

> The UK manager came from 'professional', non-business stock, whereas the US manager was more likely to have parents with blue collar occupations. Additionally 18% of US managers had parents who ran their own business, in sharp contrast to the UK manager, not one of whom came from a small business background. Indeed, the overall picture suggests an American

path of upward social mobility, whereas the parents of British top managers had already achieved that echelon of social status. Movement in British social class groupings is slow, perpetuating the elite.

The situation seems a little different with our data. Overall, we found no class bias in our sample, with about half the sample describing their origins as either working class or middle class. In terms of occupation of the father twenty-two fathers were professional or managerial, nineteen were blue-collar workers and four were low-status, white-collar workers (unskilled clerical jobs). However, most of those with professional or managerial backgrounds were heading the very large corporations, mainly in the London area. Those whose fathers were blue-collar workers were mainly to be found in the smaller engineering companies in the North-West.

Childhood Events

Eight of our sample had suffered the death of their father when they were under the age of 16. Ten others were, however, separated from their parents at an early age. This was usually either through being sent away to boarding-school at a very young age, or through being evacuated during the Second World War. Sometimes the former was due to the latter. One important factor in the lives of this particular age group is that the war came at a formative stage in their development. One other side-effect of this is that fathers were often away for long periods. Of those who were brought up by both parents in a normal home environment, twenty-two could identify events or other factors in their childhood which seemed significant in relation to their subsequent success. This leaves only five who could identify nothing of importance in childhood.

Separation

Obviously one of the most traumatic forms of separation for a child is the death of a parent. As noted above, eight of our sample had experienced this. (All were, in fact, fathers; none reported the death of their mother.) The effect of this seems to have been to develop an early sense of responsibility, the child, particularly if the eldest son, moving into a role as head of the family.

> I suppose the effect of my father dying was probably most significant. He was a solicitor. We were fairly comfortably off. After he died, because solicitors do not have much to sell I more or less had to look after myself financially, and to some extent my mother and sister as well.

This person's father died when the boy was 15. Other people thought that their father's death had an effect on their personality through changing family relationships, particularly the removal of male influence and an increased influence from their mother.

> My father died when I was very young [aged 8]. I did not have a man alongside me – just Mother and three sisters. From the age of 8 I did not have a man to turn to. So from that point of view it determined my character – made me, I suppose, a bit more aggressive, because I was in a woman's world . . . . It provided a lot of steel inside me.

For several others, the separation was due to being sent to boarding-school at an early age, one (in the case quoted below) being as young as 3 years old. Quite often, boarding-school was started at the age of 8. Most of those to whom this had happened referred to it as a significant event, which tended to make them more independent and able to cope with life on their own.

> A dominant feature of my childhood, if I am honest about it, is the fact that I went away to school. I first went away, as a

weekly boarder, not very far from home, at the age of 3½. At the age of 8 I went to a prep school and then on to a public school. I don't think I have any complexes about this, but I can't help feeling that it must have had a profound effect, particularly as I have a younger brother and sister and we all went to different schools. So we did not have the close-knit, standard family childhood. We had, I think, in retrospect a rather fragmented childhood . . . .

It really was dominant – going back to school, then you really were on your own.

Interestingly, this individual gave 'independence' as one of his motivators, and talked about himself as 'detached'. Sometimes it was the war which necessitated going away to school:

I was born in Ceylon and at the age of 7 sent home to a prep school. This was at the start of the war, so I did not really see my parents again for nine years . . . . I boarded during the holidays in a place with three or four other expat children. We were very much left to our own devices. I also did not very much like school. I had to learn to operate very indpendently.

Sometimes it was simply evacuation in this country which had the same effect:

I was evacuated to a school sixty miles from home. This gave me a measure of independence and self-reliance. Six months after returning home, I was away in the army. So, effectively, I left home at 11.

In one case only was the separation caused by a broken home:

I come from a broken home. My parents separated when I was at an early age. I was determined to show the world that I could do as well as others . . . . I was very independent. I learned to look after myself from the age of 5.

Detachment

In other cases, the sense of separation arose neither from the death of a parent nor from being sent away at an early age, but from feelings of loneliness and detachment, arising, usually, from being an only child.

> I am an only child, which in a way I regretted, because there were great periods of loneliness. But I often used to find myself in those periods of loneliness, I guess, thinking up great ideas. They would probably have never worked. I was quite imaginative – not in an artistic sense, but in many other ways.

This was heightened, in at least one case, by a feeling of distance because the father was elderly.

> I am an only child and my father was quite elderly when I was born. My mother was much younger. My relationship with my father was rather remote. He was very Victorian . . . . I was very independent as a child. I would describe myself as a loner – self-contained.

Parental Influence

The popular conception of the 'ambitious parent', moulding and encouraging the child, would seem to have been at least partially true for some of our sample of MDs: 'I think it was made pretty clear to me, and my brother, that we were expected to do well. We were both fairly successful, in work and games.' In other cases, a high value was clearly placed on achievement: 'My parents valued achievement. This was a motivation to do better. There was always a ready recognition of achievement. This was a key thing in my childhood.' Although many people mentioned this type of factor, no one seemed to see it as having produced very strong pressures in their childhood. It came over, mainly, as an expectation that they would do well, but from supportive and caring parents: 'My parents probably were ambitious for me. They certainly did all they could to fund an education . . . . There was no strong pressure – just an expectation that I ought to be getting on with things;'

Origins, Childhood and Education

There were, of course, a number of other childhood influences mentioned, apart from those of parents. These were mainly connected with school or other organized activities.

> One thing which taught me, I think, some of the joys of management – handling people – getting things accomplished through other people, which is, roughly, what management is about, in many ways, apart from having your own abilities. At a very early age – this was, of course, during the war – I joined the army cadet force – my local one. I rose rapidly through the ranks and thoroughly enjoyed the whole thing – really enjoyed it. Now this may sound very farcical, but you could not join the school cadet force until you were in the fifth form. I was already a sergeant instructor by then, and so my form mates were rookies and I already had rank, and so I had to overcome that. I think, if you can, at that age, get those guys to go along with you and not resent you, and still play cricket with them, you had to exercise an awful lot of skills. I think that that was when I found that I had skills to deal with these situations.

This type of event constituted only a small proportion of the influences mentioned.

Escape from Poverty

As will be mentioned later, in chapter 4, some MDs referred to money as an important motivator in their early life, although all of them said it was no longer an important factor. It is not, however, surprising that some of these same individuals should suggest that an important factor in their early life was a financially impoverished background – 'Through the thirties we were perilously short of money, all the time, which, I think, probably emerges as a strong motivation' – or again:

> When I visit my home environment – now very run down – as we are leaving I usually say to my wife, 'I am glad that I escaped from that environment.' It was the fear of ever returning to it that was one of the spurs. It really is the fear of being poor again which is a great motivator.

It should be mentioned that only a small proportion of the sample had experienced early poverty. The majority recorded that they were quite comfortably off in childhood; in objective terms, they varied from financially adequate to quite wealthy. However, for that minority it was an important motivating factor.

The Effects of Childhood Experience

It should be stressed that, almost universally, respondents saw their childhood as normal and happy. Even those whose fathers had died or who had been separated from their parents said this quite spontaneously. The other factors only tended to emerge during further discussion. In line with the findings of other studies, notably Cooper and Hingley's *The Change Makers*, one of the key factors in childhood does seem to be a feeling of separation. This was mentioned by about half the sample. This was mainly due to the death of the father or being sent away from home for some reason. The effect of this seems to have been to produce an early feeling of independence and self-reliance. By contrast with Cooper and Hingley's findings, however, most respondents did not see themselves as 'loners'; on the contrary, the majority reported that they were very gregarious and as children had many friends. The two samples are, of course, different in emphasis, although they overlap. Cooper and Hingley were studying individuals responsible for major change, many of whom were corporate chairmen or trade-union general secretaries.

Some three-quarters of the sample could identify something in their parents' attitude or approach to their upbringing which seemed a significant influence in their subsequent success. Perhaps not surprisingly, this was usually an attitude which valued 'achievement and success', or encouraged 'enterprise and independence'. Only a small minority mentioned early poverty as a spur to success.

A final word of warning should be added to this section. The above findings should obviously be treated with some caution – as indeed, should the findings of other similar studies. We do not, of course, always know whether other, less successful, groups in the community also have similar background events in childhood. In some cases, they obviously do. Many children come from financially deprived backgrounds. They do not all become successful managing directors, or successful at anything else. Many children of this generation were separated from their parents by evacuation during the war. While these are, obviously, very significant events, what is important is not the event itself, but how the individual responds to it. This is the result of a complex set of factors, still not clearly understood. What does seem to be the case for this group, and other similar ones which have been studied, is that the way in which they responded and successfully coped with these situations set a pattern for successfully coping with other events throughout life.

> *The effect of childhood experiences on major change makers*
>
> Memories of loss, whether of person or place, and feelings of insecurity, were recalled vividly, and often with emotion, by many of the group and were often held to be a signficant factor in their later development. Psychologists might see these early adverse experiences as likely to be traumatic, literally 'wounding' to the developing personality. Yet, as the physical wound produces healthy scar tissue often stronger than normal to protect the damaged area, so the personality may protect itself by defending vulnerable aspects of the psyche in similar ways, by compensating through a number of defence mechanisms. Certainly a number of those we interviewed reported feelings of *strength through adversity*. This was often guided and directed by some 'significant other person' to the achievement of some positive goals. Early traumas seem to have resulted in a successful testing out of their 'survival skills', a 'psychic tempering', leading to a basic feeling of strength, self-sufficiency and independence, which would serve them well in their later careers.
> C. L. Cooper and P. Hingley, *The Change Makers*, Harper & Row, London, 1985)

Education

A number of studies – by Channon, Margerison, Kakabadse and Margerison, Norburn, and others – have shown a connection between higher levels of education and the attainment of senior management or chief executive status, in both the UK and the United States. There is, however, quite a substantial variation between the studies' findings on the percentage of managers who had achieved various levels of education. Margerison found that 65 per cent of British chief executive officers had at least a first degree, compared with 86 per cent in America. Norburn and Birley, in a sample of 953 senior executives in the USA, found that 63 per cent had a first degree; of these 57 per cent were science degrees, 33 per cent arts degrees and 9 per cent business degrees. A survey carried out by the *Wall Street Journal* in 1987 found the highest level of education of American CEOs to be: high school 6 per cent, university 46 per cent, master's degree 35 per cent and doctorate 13 per cent; This implies that 94 per cent of this sample had at least a first degree, assuming that 'university education' actually means graduating.

It is interesting to compare the above figures with the results of our survey. Somewhat less than half the group (eighteen in all) had university degrees. Two of these had PhDs and two others had other postgraduate qualifications. Three had started university courses but had not completed them. The remaining twenty-four had all left school between the ages of 14 and 16. Eight had attended public schools; the rest had gone to grammar schools (the average age of the group was such that most had received their schooling before the days of comprehensive and secondary modern schools). There was, as might be expected, a fairly strong trend for those who had attended university to be from professional backgrounds, but this was not universal.

Most of those who, after leaving school, pursued no further full-time education either took up apprenticeships (usually in engineering) or entered professional offices (most usually in accountancy) and continued their education via evening classes, finishing with membership of various professional bodies, such as AMIMechE or ACA. Several of the graduates also went on to gain professional qualifications. Table 2.1 shows the range of qualifications possessed by the MDs in the sample. It can be seen that engineering and accountancy qualifications are the two largest single groups, with arts degrees being quite well represented. Of those who had either degrees or professional qualifications, 22 per cent were in engineering, 22 per cent in accountancy, 29 per cent could be loosely grouped as being in science and 27 per cent were in the arts or law.

Two things surprised us slightly about the educational background of this group. Six people had reached the level of managing director of quite large concerns without any formal qualifications. We were also slightly surprised by the number of non-graduates. We suspect this may be due to the age group concerned. We would expect the next generation moving into these positions to show a higher proportion of graduates, as

TABLE 2.1 Range of managing directors' qualifications

Area of qualification	No. in group
Engineering (graduate and professional)	9
Accountancy (ICA and ICMA)	9
Chemistry	5
Textiles (degree)	2
Law (graduate and professional)	4
Pharmacy	1
Physics	2
Metallurgy	1
Printing and design	1
Arts (degree; mainly modern languages and history)	7
No qualification	6

N.B. Some people had more than one qualification.

the trend to continue into higher education increases. What these results do suggest, however, is that higher education is not a prerequisite for success in industry. In fact, one man saw it as a positive disadvantage, commenting that he had gained a five-year lead in experience over graduates by leaving school at 16 and starting work. The percentage continuing to higher education is also significantly lower than in the studies quoted above. One reason for this may be that the other studies were all carried out by means of postal questionnaires, and possibly, in that case, there is a tendency to obtain a higher rate of response from those with higher levels of qualification.

Our data also provides only limited support for the belief that British industry is dominated by engineers and accountants – in our group, only eighteen out of the forty-five (40 per cent). Quite a number of the companies involved were, in fact, headed by someone whose original qualification was in no way related to the technology or product involved. Another popular piece of mythology is that top British management is dominated by public-school, Oxbridge graduates. Norburn provides some support for this view. In *The Chief Executive*, which compared the backgrounds and characteristics of chief executive officers (CEO) and the rest of the top management team (TMT), he found that, 'Whereas Cambridge failed to differentiate between the two sets, both Oxford and London skewed strongly towards the CEO. Conversely the older provincial universities – Manchester, Glasgow and Birmingham – showed prominance for the TMT.' In our sample, just under half the graduates (ten) came from Oxford (seven) or Cambridge (three). But, again, there was a strong bias in the distribution, most of the Oxbridge graduates being in the large companies in the South. This is at variance with the findings of Heller, reported in the *Sunday Times*, that of the heads of seventeen of the largest and most famous British companies most were graduates, but only two were Oxbridge. Again, in our sample, the Oxbridge graduates were, with two exceptions, from public schools. The implication is that large companies in the South are run by public-school/Oxbridge graduates, while the Northern companies are run by ex-grammar-school boys with degrees from provincial universities or professional qualifications.

Summary

Our data show that there are two main streams in terms of social background and education among the managing directors that we sampled. There is one group from professional backgrounds with public-school and Oxbridge educations. There is a somewhat larger group from predominantly lower socio-economic backgrounds, who have attended grammar schools and provincial universities, or taken up articles or apprenticeships leading to professional qualifications. There is a distinct bias among the Oxbridge men towards the larger, London-based companies, and among the others towards smaller, Northern-based companies. In fact, there is, for this generation of Oxbridge men, a bias completely away from industry. Several mentioned during the interviews that they had taken up industrial jobs only after failing to gain entry to the diplomatic or senior civil service. There were a number of individuals who stood out against all these trends, including a significant minority who had no formal qualifications. In general, there is some evidence that the social base of Britain's top executives is widening – which is consistent with Heller's view.

What cannot be determined from our survey is the likely effect of various changes in our educational system. The start on the path to success had, for many of the group, been a traditional grammar-school education. These schools, effectively, no longer exist. Will the comprehensive system provide the same opportunities for the next generation? We will not know until they arrive at senior managerial positions. Another factor is the formation of the business schools and the relatively recent development of MBA education in Britain. As discussed in the next chapter, only four MDs had an MBA or equivalent. Will this be different for the next generation? Will an MBA become a necessity for managerial promotion, as assumed by most business schools? If so, this means that an academic background will be a necessity too. Such a development could also produce a bias back towards a professional background. Whitley, Thomas and Marceau point out in *Masters of Business* that the fathers of 90 per cent of the students at the London and Manchester Business Schools were, or had been, engaged in non-manual occupations, usually of a professional, administrative or managerial nature. Alternatively, will there always be, as Heller implies, room for the competent and assertive individual to fight his way up?

The other main theme of this chapter has been the effect of childhood experience and parental influence on later success. There is moderately strong evidence, consistent with Cooper and Hingley's findings, that early self-sufficiency and responsibility is an important factor. This seems to be associated with feelings of aloneness and/or separation from parents. This can be caused by a number of factors – the death of a parent, particularly the father; being sent to boarding-school at an early age; being an only child; or, in the case of the age group in question, being evacuated during the war. There is some, but not strong, evidence that parental expectations and encouragement are important. Financial motivation was mentioned by a small minority, but seems relatively unimportant. It is possible that this is influenced by the social undesirability of admitting to being motivated by money.

3
CAREER DEVELOPMENT

Only very recently, in the second half of the twentieth century, has management been seen as anything approaching a profession with any sort of career structure or formal training. Prior to that, as Whitley, Thomas and Marceau put it in *Masters of Business*, 'British managers, like British gentlemen, were born rather than made, and management itself had been seen principally as an art learnt by long years of practical experience in the workplace rather than in the groves of academe.' In fact, management has, in general, been seen as a legitimate academic study in the UK only for the last twenty years. The two first business schools (at London and Manchester) were set up in the mid-1960s, although there were some university management departments before this, most notably that at UMIST. Business schools have, of course, been a feature of American universities for rather longer.

Three recent reports on management development suggest that the situation has not really, even now, changed in practice. Constable and McCormick, in *The Making of British Managers*, a report for the British Institute of Management, found that, of the 90,000 entering management roles each year, most have no formal management training. Those already in management posts receive, on average, one day of training per year. It is stressed that this is an average and conceals a wide variation. C. B . Handy, in a comparative study of managers in five countries (Britain, Japan, the USA, France and West Germany), found that British managers received far less business education than managers in the other countries. He suggests that 'Management in Britain has traditionally been more to do with pragmatism than professionalism. Common sense, character and background have been throughout more important than education, and experience the only worthwhile school.' The third report, *Developing Directors* by Mumford, Robinson and Stradling, concerns a survey of 144 directors from a wide range of British companies. Again, the finding is that most directors have had little or no formal training or, in fact, any form of career development. Their learning came mainly from job experience, and their perception was that the main influence on their career progression was 'being in the right place at the right time', although most directors did claim the ability to 'seize and take advantage' of these accidental events.

Kakabadse and Margerison, in a report of a survey of 711 American CEOs, which they compare with an earlier study by Margerison of British chief executives, observe that becoming the head of a major company sems to be a very personal 'developmental process', independent of the organization or educational system:

> The results seem to suggest that CEOs see themselves, first, as individuals who have worked hard, hold unique styles and approaches to managing, and are sincerely attempting to act on their responsibilities toward the organisation and its employees. Their credibility and successful performance do not stem from the fact that they are corporate people who follow a corporate line. In fact, the tension between personal views and corporate 'ways of doing things' causes frequent difficulties. Rather, they are people who have achieved success by developing their skills – in dealing with people and organisational problems.

The picture that emerges from these reports is one of management development in reality continuing to be a matter of pragmatic experience. The academic endeavour of the last twenty years seems to have had little impact. Management is still not widely viewed as a profession, needing formal training and qualification. This is totally consistent with the backgrounds of the managing directors we interviewed.

Career Patterns

In his 1958 study, *Managers*, R. V. Clements identified five basic patterns in managerial careers:

The crown Prince. He or she is a member of the family owning the business

The ex-managerial trainee. He or she is usually a university graduate recruited specifically to be trained for, ultimately, a managerial position.

The expert trained before entering industry. These are people who enter industry after taking specialist training and qualifications, most often in accountancy. They tend to be promoted, initially, in their specialized area, but may transfer into general management later in their careers.

The special entrant. This is a somewhat miscellaneous category of people who did not fit the other classifications. They include sales trainees, specialist apprentices and those who have negotiated some special form of entry to a company.

Rising from the bottom. These are people who have literally started their careers at the lowest level of the organization, often as either clerks or manual workers.

In the thirty years since Clements' study there have been considerable changes in society and in the educational system, and this makes it hard to make direct comparisons. Perhaps surprisingly, 'crown princes' still exist. Two MDs in our sample had succeeded their fathers in the same position. One was in a direct line of descent from four previous generations; the other took over a small firm started by his father and built it into a large public company. A third MD did belong to the family which had originally started a company that is now part of a very large, publicly owned group. While it would, undoubtedly, have been an advantage to bear the family name, particularly early in his career, it is unlikely that he would have reached his present position without competition from outside candidates. He probably belongs, more properly, in the category of 'special entrant'.

By far the largest group in our sample could be classified as 'special entrants' – at least half, if we include all those who do not fit the other categories. However, because of the social changes noted above, this is a very different group from that defined by Clements. National service is one important factor. Because of the age group we are dealing with (mainly 50–60, with a few in their late forties), most of the sample had military experience. (Some had been exempt while doing research or on medical grounds.) Although nearly all of them saw this as significant experience, only three went straight to junior management jobs after university degrees and national service commissions. The largest subgroup within the 'special entrant' category (thirteen in all) started as apprentices of one sort or another. These range from craft apprentices who went on to graduate or to professional qualifications, through clerical workers and laboratory assistants taking day-release and evening courses for professional qualifications, to university graduates taken on for further technical training under graduate apprenticeship schemes.

The next largest group, consisting of fifteen people, can be classified as 'experts trained before entering'. These consisted of seven scientists, whose first job was in most cases in research, and eight accountants and lawyers, who trained and spent some time in professional practice before entering industry. Five of the sample started as 'management trainees'. Only one MD could truly be said to have 'risen from the bottom'. This man had left school without qualifications of any kind, and his first job was a lorry driver's mate. He took some accountancy courses during national service, but, lacking the necessary entry qualifications, was unable to continue to membership of any of the professional bodies. After military service he took a job as a cost clerk, worked his way steadily to become managing director of the UK division of a large multinational company, and is now on the board of the American parent company.

There are a few individuals who cannot realistically be classified into any of the above categories. For example, one man spent twenty years as an officer in the Royal Engineers before moving into a civilian management career. Another spent one year working in the family company and then left to start his own business, which was subsequently bought up by a large group; he is now MD of a group of companies which was part of that conglomerate. Finally, one man qualified as a chemist and, while working as a research chemist, studied part-time for accountancy qualifications. He then became a technical sales trainee and spent some years in the sales function before moving to more senior general management.

Career Progression

It is obvious from the above that the ways in which managing directors enter their careers are very varied, and probably defy classification. There are, however, a number of characteristics which their careers have in common and which are, therefore, probably significant. All of them had moved around a great deal. In their early careers, they tended to spend very little time in any one job – usually only two or three years. This time tended to increase as they reached more senior positions.

Most had experience of more than one company. Only six (including the three 'crown princes') had spent their whole career with one organization; in the case of four of them, this was a very large multinational, within which there was scope for considerable movement and experience of different functions and operations. Considering those who had changed company, it is hard to detect any particular patterns. Some made one or two job changes (involving a change of company) early on, and then settled with a larger organization, gradually working their way to the top. Others had changed company very frequently, only settling with their present organization relatively later in their careers. In yet other cases, almost every 'job move' involved a change of employer. In some cases, the final move to managing-director level involved a change to a new organization. Quite often this was as a result of an approach from a firm of 'head hunters'. For two men this final move was as a result of a management buy-out.

Wide Experience

Whatever the pattern of moves, whether within one organization or across many, one thing in common was that their careers included a wide breadth of experience involving many functions and often a range of product types. One man summarized his career as follows:

> I started in accountancy and rose to a reasonable level. I was then promoted into a job which was, largely, sales and customer oriented. Next, I moved into a company which was very much manufacturing oriented, and I felt, at the end of that time, that I was probably rounded off and ready for a more senior position – I had finished my apprenticeship. I moved to become MD of a large manufacturing subsidiary of a large group and then to my present job. (chief executive of a medium-size group)

Sometimes this experience was gained by working at a more senior level in a small company. The following comment concerns experience as the assistant to the MD of such a company.

> It gave me wide experience. I ran everything – accounts, sales, the factory. Looking back, I think it is one of the better things I did, because I saw business in all its aspects. You don't get this in big companies.

Career Development

This approach also has the advantage of giving experience of 'top management', as well as of a range of functions. Many of the sample had been managing director of a small subsidiary quite early in their careers.

Another aspect of experience, in which most of our sample were involved, was that of working abroad. This was considered to be important in terms of broadening outlook and developing the ability to cope with new situations.

> Working abroad is important. It widens experience. Staying in England, one can become very insular. Working abroad, you encounter new cultures and cope with new problems.

Early Responsibility

Several writers have noted that successful managers achieve positions of responsibility at an early age. In large organizations with many layers of management, this is obviously essential if an individual is to reach the top, and it was a characteristic of the managers in our group. Frequently, however, there was an extra dimension – almost of 'make or break'. Many of them had been given an assignment with complete responsibility and very little outside support. Often this was to manage an overseas subsidiary, where they were very much on their own and had to cope. Most saw this as a key development experience, as one CEO reported:

> There have been one or two influences, in a way lucky and in a way creative. Early in my career with [named company], when I was a scientist, I was sent on a company executive course. I think I was the first taken out of the labs on to one of these, and apparently I shone. So, although it was not in my own planned career, I was asked to come out of the labs and take a managerial job. Now that was a fundamental change . . . .
>
> The next fundamental change was after about three years in management when [the company] shipped me to Africa – before I was 30 – to become the general manager of an operation in

Africa. Now this, in itself, was a tremendous aid to career development, because you are isolated from the civilized world and you have to know about management, and about marketing, and about manufacturing, and you have to be able to lead, and to do . . . .

I learnt, mainly, from doing a job in an environment where I was allowed to manage at a relatively young age.

In another example:

When I was about 29 I went to a conglomerate which was a shambles from beginning to end. It had a 92-year-old chairman and there was a void in management. Suddenly, overnight, I found myself plunged into this situation where, quite literally, you were allowed to do anything you were prepared to do, the void was so big. I ended up, very rapidly, looking after five of the subsidiaries.

Another respondent had at the age of 24, and just after the war, been made solely responsible for developing sales throughout the whole of Europe. In other cases, individuals had been given responsibility for 'turning round' unprofitable parts of the organization. What is significant is that they had all been successful in the assignments given. What we do not know is what happens to those for whom such opportunities do not work out.

Risk and Challenge

Closely associated with early responsibility was the fact that most of the sample had accepted challenges and taken calculated risks during their careers. In chapter 6 it is noted that most chief executives regarded themselves as moderate risk-takers, but because of their confidence, both in their ability to calculate the risk and in their skill in dealing with it, they did not see the risks as unduly high. Much the same thinking is evident in their approach to their careers. Many of them had, at some stage, taken on the challenge of 'turning round' an ailing subsidiary. One man, for example, described how he had been

Career Development

appointed to sort out a problem company. The attraction was complete control and authority. The negative side was a redundancy programme involving 40 per cent of the workforce, but he found high satisfaction in returning the company to profit.

> It was extremely satisfying, looking back, but also very unpleasant at times. The other thing which attracted me was that one never knows if one is capable of doing a thing like that until one tries it, and if you do, as I did, and it succeeds, it is enormously satisfying. It has been the most satisfying part of my career, there's no question about that, because I feel I have done it on my own . . . .
> I did not see it as a risk. I felt pretty confident and I had researched the background. I felt pretty confident I could put it right.

Interestingly, quite often in a situation like this, the individual had discussed with his family (both wife and children) the risks involved and had reached a joint decision with them that the chance was worth taking. This was because failure would, obviously, also affect the family.

Other individuals saw their career as a series of challenges, each new job developing and improving their skills:

> I think how my career has developed is that you get given a job to do, at a level. You struggle with it until you master it, and then you are comfortable with it. Then you move up a peg to a level with a wider span of responsibility and the same thing happens all over again. You struggle with it again because it is bigger. You are able to cope again because of the experience you gained at the lower level, and you develop experience at the new from contact with colleagues and the work itself. You are constantly moving your abilities up.

Luck and Chance

When asked about their careers, the initial response of many people was to attribute it to luck.

Never overlook the effect of luck, of being in the right place at the right time. There is also the effect of being in an expanding company, compared with a contracting situation.

Further discussion usually showed, however, that this was only part of the story. Most people had experienced some lucky breaks, but it was also necessary to have the ability to capitalize on them. The old adage, 'It is surprising how much my luck improves when I work hard', probably applies. It also seems to be necessary to make sure you are seen and known to be capable and ambitious, as one top MD explained:

> I have manipulated my progress in this company, because I have used things like appraisal systems when I had something to say to the management of the company. I think one of the biggest problems I have is to persuade people to tell me their aspirations. If you want to get into the main line of the business, you had better day so. But I have been lucky on a couple of occasions.

The effect of the Second World War appears again in this context, as expressed in the following remarks:

> Luck must to some extent enter into any career. It's a cliché, I know, but being in the right place at the right time is important. I think my generation and people of my age [55] in a variety of industries benefited from two things. One is the tragedy that a lot of people did not come back from the war, and, secondly, after the war there was pretty substantial growth. Certainly in this industry we had growth rates of 10, 12, 14 per cent per year, and suddenly you were having to commission new plants and you had no one with experience. So what did you do? You threw in the young men that you had. So my generation, in fact, were dropped in at the deep end, and a reasonable number of us, after a while, did swim . . . .
> Now the competition is greater and the situation has changed. We don't promote people, now, as quickly as in my generation. The economy has slowed down and plants are bigger. There are more problems if things go wrong. Therefore, there is more need for qualifications.

Career Development

There is also an echo here of the developmental effect of 'early responsibility' and the necessity of finding one's own salvation. A similar view, but in a different context, was put forward by an arts graduate who had spent his career in a chemical company; the comment of this CEO illustrates the joint effect of luck and industry:

> The good thing about my early years with the company is that I was absolutely useless to them. Therefore, I had to get on and learn something, learn about the business and move around and teach myself things. The people I feel sorry for are the good chemists we get in, who stay at the bench for the rest of their lives. One of the reasons for that is that they have an immediate utility.

Career Planning

If people see their careers as to some extent influenced by luck, one would not expect to find much evidence of deliberate career planning. This did, indeed, prove to be the case. While most of the sample were ambitious men, they did not admit to an early desire to become a managing director or claim to have mapped out, in any detail, their future career paths. Success was more a matter of attending to the job in hand and doing it well. This approach was described by one person as follows:

> I am not particularly ambitious. My present position is a consequence of many events, each building upon the other. One can't put one's head in the sand – in thinking about life one has got to look at the possibilities for the future – but I think, if an executive is very carefully mapping out his progress as to when he wants to be where, at what age, at what time, etc., then, in my opinion, the probabilities are that he will never make it, because along the way he will probably be devoting insufficient time to what he is, in fact, being paid to do at that time. The guy who's got his head down, doing an excellent job, is more likely to be the one who gets the tap on the shoulder and is offered the more senior position.

Another man expressed very similar views, but did make the point that he would have taken action, if he had felt that all was not going well, at any particular time.

> That, basically, is the way my career developed and, as you can see, there was not any planning to it. It was doing a job and doing it well, I suppose, in the hope that somebody might think I was doing it well, and might think I was suitable for doing something more important, and thats the way it worked out . . . .
>
> Had I felt stuck at any point, I would have started to look for a new job to widen my experience, but I always got change and promotion.

Management Development

There has been a debate for a long time, among both academics and managers, over the value of management training. Opinions have differed, not only about the value of academic programmes such as MBAs and business degrees, but also about the more practical training provided by most large organizations – managers, in general, being fairly sceptical about all forms of management development. There have also been a number of formal studies of the effect of management training. J. S. Livingston, for example, in his article on 'The myth of the well-educated manager', found no correlation between grades in either undergraduate or postgraduate business courses and subsequent success in management. Other studies, such as that by Weinstein and Srinivasan, have found significant correlations between MBA grades and subsequent levels of earning. Data from the business schools also confirm this trend. But the fact that business-school graduates obtain better-paid jobs does not mean they are better managers; on the contrary, it may be because they tend to go to professional or service-based occupations (e.g. investment banking) rather than managerial jobs.

It has already been noted that British managers do not, in

any case, receive much formal management development. A. Mumford found, for instance, that most directors had learnt through job experience and did not identify training programmes as important in their development (in Mumford, Robinson and Stradling, *Developing Directors*). Against this background, it is interesting and significant to find that very few of our sample of MDs had any formal management training. Most had been on various short courses (two or three days up to a week) on a variety of specialist topics, such as accounting or marketing. Apart from this, only four had attended an MBA programme or its equivalent, and one had taken a diploma in management studies. Three people had attended shorter business-school courses, of between six and eight weeks' duration. Thus only eight out of the forty-five had attended any long-term formal training – and three of these for only a few weeks!

This is, at first sight, very surprising and disappointing, in view of the high level of activity in management courses in universities and polytechnics. It is partly explained, however, by the age of the sample. Since these are men who are now at the top of organizations, their formative years were during the 1950s and early 1960s, when there were not so many management courses available in the UK. It will unfortunately also be due to the negative view of management education discussed above. High-flyer managers get on and do things. They do not spend time on training programmes. If there is some specific knowledge or skill which they require, they go to a short course dealing with that specific topic. It is probable that the next generation of top managers will have more formal training, since there is now so much of it available. There is some evidence for this, in that it was mainly the younger members of the group who had the formal management qualifications.

The fact remains, however, that this group had, in the main, succeeded as managers without the benefit of formal training. Whether they would have been better managers with this we do not, of course, know. Their own opinion is that it would

> *The British approach*
>
> Management in Britain has traditionally been more to do with pragmatism than professionalism. Common sense, character and background have been throughout more important than education, and experience the only worthwhile school. However the complexity of modern business and the rising levels of both education and expectation among younger managers have brought demands for a swing towards professionalism. Management as a skill has come to be increasingly valued
>
> At present there are only two semi-professional routes into business: Accountancy and joining the big corporation and using it as a Business School. In Britain you do some basic study, take a qualification examination to enter a profession (but not to practise), then a period of organised apprenticeship and then finally you get qualified and 'off you go'.
>
> Charles [Handy] suggests 'that there are only three important roles in Britain for which you need no qualification or training—being a parent, a politician or a manager. (Some would say that we do not do any of them well enough')
>
> (From a review in the *Association for Management Education and Development News* of the report by Charles Handy, *The Making of Managers: a report on management education, training and development in the United States, West Germany, France, Japan and the UK*, National Economic Development Council, London, 1987)

not have made much difference. Even those with the formal training did not in general see it as very useful. The common comment was that it was the informal discussion with fellow delegates which was most useful, together with the contacts made. It should be recorded that two managers did see it as providing a valuable background on which they could build, with later experience. In these cases, the education probably provided a conceptual framework and tools for analysis. The lack of this was bemoaned by some of those who had not continued far through the formal educational system, as illustrated by one of our MDs:

Career Development

> I may have a chip on my shoulder about university (i.e. not having been to one) but I don't feel that at any time in my educational experience my mind has been trained to think – really to think. I have not got a trained mind for thinking in stages and then producing an argument. I find that a serious lack, in my present position. I am fortunate in that I have a fair measure of common sense and I can fudge my way through, but I think a lack of formal education, or formal thinking process, is a weakness that I have.

The above was very much a minority view. By and large, the MDs in this sample were much more in favour of learning from experience, perhaps because, as noted above, this is what they had actually had to do.

Mentors

Since successful managers do not necessarily have formal management training, their skills must be acquired 'on the job'. Consequently, we were interested in what help or support they may have had with this, and we asked them if they could identify people who had acted as mentors during their career. The answer was usually 'yes'. Often several were mentioned. These usually turned out to be an immediate boss at some earlier period. It was not usually a formal mentoring arrangement, but simply a good boss who provided help and guidance, as illustrated by one CEO:

> I have had no formal mentors, but I learnt a lot from one particular boss. I worked for him for five years. Looking back on it, there is no question but that what I am now, I am as a result of learning from him.

How this works, at its best, was described by someone else:

> I think the best form of management development, and career development, is to work for good managers. I have been fortunate in my career – certainly, I have worked for one outstanding manager, a man, I think, who was brilliant. He was extremely demanding, a first-class manager, astute, very

shrewd, and he had the great quality of allowing people he trusted *carte blanche*. He'd give them their head, and, I think, he got as much pleasure watching them develop as the individuals did themselves.

There were a few cases of more formal mentoring systems:

I am a great believer in the mentor principle. Two mentors have been influential in my career. The first was very formal. I made a report each week and we discussed progress and planned for the future. I have implemented this system here. The second one was more informal – my immediate boss.

In general, however, it was simply a matter of learning from a respected senior, who quite possibly did not see himself as a mentor at all but was probably just being helpful to a promising junior. Two MDs who had attended business schools also mentioned academics, from whom they had learnt a lot, and whom they still used for help and advice. These had now moved from a true mentor role to that of an academic 'guru'. We were interested to note that, although most of these MDs had not themselves had formal mentors, they had, in many cases, introduced a mentoring system into their organization. Presumably, this was to try to make the benefits they felt that they had received, perhaps, by good luck, more generally available.

Successful Managerial Careers

The key ingredients for a successful managerial career would seem to be:

Wide early experience covering a range of functions and, ideally, also a range of different types of company.

Early responsibility involving complete control of a company or overseas subsidiary.

Acceptance of challenge involving risk. This is often part of the early responsibility in that the first solo assignment may well be challenging and risky. It is also an attribute which continues throughout the subsequent career. It is important that the risk is not a gamble. It is a calculated risk, which is seen to be within the reasonable limits of the manager's skills and abilities.

No overall career plan, but being ready and willing to take opportunities as they arise.

Learning from experience, helped by a good boss.

These findings are consistent with much of the literature on management careers. Norburn and Birley found that chief executives showed both wider functional and greater breadth of company experience than other members of the top management team. Kakabadse and Margerison draw attention to the width of experience of chief executives: American CEOs had, on average, worked for 3.6 separate organizations and held 7.8 categorically different jobs; in the UK survey, the figures were 2.9 organizations and 8.1 separate jobs. McCall and Lombardo, comparing successful executives ('arrivers') with those who had started with promise but failed along the way ('derailed'), found that

> Derailed executives had a series of successes, but usually in similar situations. They had turned a business around more than once, or they had managed progressively larger jobs, but in the same function. By contrast the arrivers had more diversity in their successes – they had turned a business around *and* successfully moved from line to staff and back: or they had started a new business from scratch *and* completed a special assignment with distinction. They built plants in the wilderness and the amazon jungle, salvaged disastrous operations, resolved all-out wars between functions without bloodshed – one even built a town.

This diversity is very reminiscent of the chief executives in our sample and does, of course, give them a very wide range of experience and opportunities for learning.

The converse effect to this width of experience is referred to by D. Q. Mills in *The New Competitors* as the *fast track trap*:

> movement across businesses and functions may be important for an individual if he or she is to avoid the fast track trap. That is, the rapid advance up the hierarchy in a narrow function or in a single business may leave the ambitious executive high up the corporate ladder but plateaued by specialisation and not acceptable in a general management position.

Mills suggests that it is the responsibility of higher management to ensure that this does not happen to ambitious juniors, and that career planning is essential to ensure that individuals know where they stand.

> Sometimes high potential people become impatient of their rate of advance; they fear they have been forgotten or intentionally passed over when others are promoted. The result may be valuable managers who watch the score board and not the game – who cease to be vitally involved and committed to their current assignments.

This echoes the views of some of our MDs, who stressed the need to concentrate on the job in hand and not keep worrying about future promotion.

Another theme from the literature, reflected in our interviews, is the importance of early experience. Cooper and Hingley note that many of their major 'change makers' started from nowhere, and they go on to observe:

> They were fortunate enough to have experienced early responsibility, which provided them with the opportunity for success or failure, development or stagnation. These opportunities were used to develop their entrepreneurial abilities in the reality of the workplace.

In *The Chief Executive and Business Growth*, G. Copeman found that chief executives considered that social skills were one of their most important assets, and that these skills too were acquired early; 28 per cent of his sample said that they had acquired confidence in the exercise of social skills by the age of 20, 76 per cent by the age of 29. Social skills were usually developed by individuals being thrown into situations where they just had to cope with other people, either at school or college, or in early work experience. Kakabadse and Margerison report very similar findings:

> It has often been said that 'management is getting things done through persuading other people'. The way to learn this is to gain a leadership post early in one's career. Most managers we have talked to feel that this experience must come before the age of 30, and preferably before the age of 25. Two thirds of all the people responding had received their first leadership command prior to the age of 30, with all but 10% being in such a position before reaching the age of 35. Perhaps the most interesting finding, however, is that 41% of all respondents had, in fact, gained their first leadership command before the age of 25.

Goldsmith and Clutterbuck found that some of the top-performing companies which they studied in *The Winning Streak* had clear policies of giving leadership experience at an early age, even to the extent of 'throwing them in at the deep end'; for example:

> STC often gives young managers their head in taking an idea to its logical conclusion as a new venture. Usually this involves a product that fits closely into the general development strategy, but occasionally young managers are allowed to develop ideas with little or no relevance to the core business, simply to expose them to practical experience of leadership in a start-up situation.

Goldsmith and Clutterbuck also draw attention to the need for 'generalized' managers. By this they mean managers with a broad background across many specialisms.

Referring to an attribute related to grasping early experience, C. Garfield remarks that peak performers are able to spot 'windows of opportunity':

> I would say peak performers use windows of opportunity to keep sight of a critical path. As they gain information and expertise in the work they do, they tell us, they develop a feel for openings, for points at which they can institute course corrections to (1) keep them within the boundaries of the critical path and (2) leap ahead.

Garfield argues that this seems to be an intuitive skill. We suspect it is also important in people's being able to make use of early opportunities and to develop the ability to be in the 'right place at the right time'.

Other writers have dealt specifically with the issue of risk in career development. In *The Boss*, Lewis and Stewart point out:

> A good business man must take risks with his career just as an entrepreneur must take risks in producing for the market. It is essential not to be overlooked, and it may be wise to refuse a good job which seems out of the main stream of promotion, and prefer something smaller which brings him in close touch with top management.

Many of the managers in our sample had fulfilled this condition of visibility with top management early in their careers by holding the position of personal assistant to the chief executive, although many of them stressed that this was not a position to stay in for too long. M. Sorcher suggests, in *Predicting Executive Success*, that the strongest candidates for chief executive come from within the organization, because their qualities are known and they have demonstrated their abilities. He does also point out that the dangers of a policy of appointing from *within* are the development of mediocrity from safe appointments and the tendency to 'inbreeding' through appointing in the image of existing top managers. It is perhaps this tendency which worried Richard Darman, Deputy Secretary of the US Treasury, in an article in the *Wall Street Journal*, in which he suggested that many American organizations showed a tendency towards 'corpocracy' and many American executives tended toward 'corpocratic grayness'. This is hopefully being avoided in the UK. Certainly our sample showed a healthy balance between promotion from within and recruitment from outside.

Management Development and Managerial Success

There are many references in the literature to the learning approaches of top managers and to the effect of mentors. In *Leaders*, Bennis and Nanus observe that 'Leaders are perpetual learners. Some are voracious readers. . . . Many learn mainly from other people . . . . Nearly all leaders are highly proficient in learning from experience. Most were able to identify a small number of mentors and key experiences that powerfully shaped their philosophies, aspirations and operating styles.' McCall and Lombardo also make the point that their 'arrivers' were 'too busy worrying about their present job to be eager for their next position, they demanded excellence from their people in problem solving and in so doing often helped develop them, and they developed many contacts, saving themselves from the sole-mentor syndrome. (In fact, almost no successful manager reported having a single mentor.)' Many of the managers we spoke to, while acknowledging the value of the learning they had gained from their immediate managers at various stages in their careers, did also stress the dangers of becoming too closely identified with the fortunes of one man. As Lewis and Stewart put it:

> One important hazard is one's immediate boss. An able superior who takes an interest in his subordinate's career can help him immensely – not least by being promoted himself . . . . A jealous or indifferent superior, and particularly one who has reached his own limit, may fatally obstruct an able junior. Valuable time may be lost by an able man blocked behind a boss who does not like him, or who does not want to lose him.

Thus another advantage of a varied career with changes of function and company is that it reduces the chances of being blocked in this way.

Mumford, Robinson and Stradling also found little evidence of formal mentoring, and only a few of the directors in their survey admitted to learning very much from former bosses, although most believed that they had probably unconsciously modelled their behaviour on that of 'admired' managers from earlier in their careers. This is slightly at odds with our findings, where many MDs identified former bosses from whom they had gained significant learning, although this was usually from everyday interaction or by osmosis, not from formal mentoring.

The most significant finding, from this and other studies, is that senior and successful managers do not learn their skills from formal development programmes but from real-life experience. While this is totally consistent with much psychological theory – most notably that of C. Rogers, who in *Freedom to Learn for the 80s* maintains that learning, to be effective, must be of immediate significance to the learner; and R. W. Revens, who in *Action Learning* argues further that effective learning must involve challenge and risk – the future of the individual must in some way be influenced by the learning situation. All this was true of the experiences recounted by the managing directors we interviewed. The problem with this approach is that it leaves much to chance, and there is evidence that some people are better able than others to learn from this type of 'real' experience. There is also the problem that the experiences themselves may be random. Many potentially good managers may not be offered the necessary early opportunities. The answer to this is that management development should include planned job changes designed to give experience that challenges the individual and develops appropriate skills. Many companies do this already in various forms, but there is room for considerable extension of this approach.

Career Development

The reports both by Handy and by Constable and McCormick call for the provision of substantially more courses on management and business studies within universities and other institutes of higher education, with, possibly, the establishment of a new management qualification – a Diploma in Business Administration – to be taken within the first few years of starting work. This is based on the finding that managers in other countries, notably the USA, Japan, France and West Germany, where there is higher productivity, are also better qualified than in the UK. In the light of the evidence about how managers actually learn, we have some doubts about the likely efficacy of this. There is no evidence that academic learning changes behaviour or develops practical skills such as those required in management. The higher productivity in other countries may well be due to other reasons.

One skill that is perhaps developed by academic training is the ability to think through a problem. This, as discussed in chapter 6, is an important and crucial ability for top managers. Some of the non-academics in our sample also bemoaned the lack of this particular form of training. Ironically, it may be that management courses, which tend to consist of a grouping of rather general courses covering a wide range of topics, are less effective at developing 'thinking skills' than the purer academic disciplines. The sort of knowledge taught on management courses – accounting, marketing, production planning, and so on – is, of course, required, but it may be better learnt from specific short courses, when the individual realizes that he has a definite need for the information.

Summary

Managing directors enter their careers from a wide variety of backgrounds and educational levels. However, as Charles Handy suggests in the report, *The Making of Managers*, there are two main routes into top management: accountancy, or working one's way up through a large corporation. This is how many of our MDs started. A few succeeded without any formal qualifications, but this is probably changing. As more of the professions require a degree as an entry qualification, and in an age when it is easier for a bright youngster to enter university, it will become less common to find senior managers who are not graduates. Whether this will have any effect on their 'skill' as managers is open to question.

In terms of career, MDs have wide experience within an range of different companies and across several functions. Early responsibility, often in a strange environment (e.g. overseas), is an important factor. This develops self-reliance and leadership qualities at an early stage. They respond to challenges and will take calculated risks with their careers. Chance probably plays a part, but our MDs were adept at creating 'good luck' and at capitalizing on opportunities. They had not usually planned their careers, and their skills were developed mainly from job experience and short courses on specific topics, taken as the need arose.

4
WORK AND MOTIVATION

The popular parody of the senior company director is of a man who is only interested in the high pay-cheque and perks of the business, and spends his time eating large and alcoholic 'expense account' meals and playing endless rounds of golf. The reality is, of course, very far from this. Most studies (including our own) have shown that top executives work very long hours. Copeman, in a survey of chief executives in three countries (the United States, Britain and Germany), found that the long hours were required to cope with the large amount of data they had to handle.

Much of the research into what motivates managers has been based on the work of A. H. Maslow (*Motivation and Personality* and F. Hertzberg (in Hertzberg, Mausner and Snyderman, *The Motivation to Work*), and it has usually shown that managers are more concerned with the higher levels of the Maslow Need Hierarchy, and with 'motivators' rather than 'hygiene' in Herzberg's terminology. For example, Haire, Ghiselli and Porter, in a large cross-cultural study, *Managerial Thinking*, found that self-realization and autonomy are universally more important to managers than are lower-level needs. D. Q. Mills, in *The New Competitors*, indicates that challenge is a key motivator for managers, but does draw attention to the importance of pay, emphasizing that it is necessary to recognize and reward performance in overcoming and responding to challenge. He also argues that top executives should see the pay system as something they manage, not something that manages them:

> rising executives must be able to see the compensation system primarily as one which they manage, not to which they are subject. They must make it work for them with regard to those who report to them – rather than being principally concerned about how it affects their own pay. They must be able to see themselves in charge of the pay system; not it in charge of them.

Hall and Donnell looked at the motivation of high, average and low achievers in management. Achievement was measured by a ratio of age to level in the organization; thus a 'high achiever' had reached very senior levels at a relatively young age, and 'low achievers' were still at the lower levels at a more advanced age. They found that the dominant motivation for high achievers was *self-actualization*, that is, a purely intrinsic motivation involving the need to use one's full capacities and to extend and develop onself. 'Average achievers' were motiviated by *ego-status needs*, that is, the need to achieve things that confirm one's status or worth. These often include external status symbols, such as the size of the office and the quality of company car provided. Presumably, high achievers are already sure of their own worth. Low achievers were concerned with *creature comforts* as well as ego-status needs. This is similar to C. Garfield's finding (in *Peak Performers*) that successful people have a sense of mission that helps them to mobilize inner resources.

The Maslow Need Hierarchy

Maslow identified five distinct need categories:
1 physiological needs;
2 safety and security needs;
3 belongingness and love needs;
4 self-esteem needs;
5 the need to self-actualize.

Work and Motivation

Furthermore, he proposed that these needs are organized into a hierarchy (see diagram below): needs higher up the hierarchy emerge to play a prominent role in the control of behaviour only when needs lower down the hierarchy are satisfied. Thus, someone who is hungry (a physiological need) will take risks and ignore safety needs to obtain food. In the work context, safety needs such as job security or safe working conditions need to be satisfied before attention is turned to the development of friendships and good relationships with others. The highest level in the hierarchy, self-actualization, concerns the needs for self-fulfillment and the achievement of one's full potential. What Maslow attempts to emphasize with his need hierarchy is the positive side of human nature, by stressing that, despite the requirement for the satisfaction of lower-level needs, humans will, whenever possible, strive to achieve their potential and attain the satisfaction that is to be derived from using one's abilities and attributes to the full.

Some possible implications of the need hierarchy for organizations are fairly clear, which may be one of the reasons why Maslow's theory has been so popular in management circles. First, the incentives or goals that will motivate employees will depend on their current level of need satisfaction. Second, it is probably in its best interest for the organization to attempt to arrange working conditions and tasks so that lower-level needs are met and employees are motivated by their own needs for self actualization.

Self-actualization
Self-esteem
Love and belongingness
Safety and security
Physiological needs

I. T. Robertson and C. L. Cooper, *Human Behaviour in Organisations*, Macdonald & Evans, London, 1983)

> *Herzberg's hygiene–motivator theory*
>
> The two-factor theory of Herzberg represents an attempt to examine the role of various job factors and how they relate to needs. His theory is based, to a large extent, on investigations of the factors in jobs that give rise to satisfaction or dissatisfaction. In an early study of a fairly small sample of engineers and accountants in the Pittsburgh area of the United States, employees were asked to describe incidents in their jobs which made them feel particularly good (satisfied) or bad (disatisfied) about them. This study and subsequent similar studies indicated those factors that were related to good feelings about the job (factors such as achievement, recognition, the work itself, responsibility) and those that were related to bad feelings (factors such as company policy and administration, working conditions, supervision). These data led Herzberg to the 'two-factor' theory, which proposes that two different types of factors contribute to satisfaction and dissatisfaction at work. Factors associated with good feelings about the job (motivators) are mostly derived from the job itself. The second set of factors (hygiene factors) are mostly external to the job and involve aspects of the physical or psychological environment. Some of the most important implications of Herzberg's theory concern the ideas about how satisfaction and motivation can be improved by restructuring or 'enriching' jobs so that they provide people with rewarding experiences.
>
> The core of Herzberg's proposal is that it will not be possible to motivate people by improving hygiene factors alone. Improvements in hygiene factors such as working conditions will perhaps decrease dissatisfaction but will not improve motivation. True motivation, according to Herzberg, derives from factors associated with the job itself and relies on offering opportunities for achievement, recognition and responsibility.
> I. T. Robertson and C. L. Cooper, *Human Behaviour in Organisations*, Macdonald & Evans, London, 1983)

It obviously takes a lot of energy and commitment to reach the level of managing director of a large organization, so it seemed worthwhile against this background to explore the orientation to work and the motivation of those who reach this position. We start by looking at their approach to work.

Work and Motivation

Work Pattern

We asked our sample to tell us what an average day was like. One problem with this, of course, is that there is really no such thing as an 'average' day, but it did emerge that all of them worked, by normal standards, quite a long day. In general, the starting time was somewhere between 8.00 to 8.30 in the morning and the finishing time in the office was not until 6.00 to 7.00 in the evening. There was quite a bit of variation around these limits, particularly in the starting time, some people starting as early as 7.00 a.m. or even 6.30. We were even offered this as the time of the interview in one case (we declined and made a later appointment!). In addition to this long day in the office, all of them took work home. Again there was considerable variation in this from individual to individual. At one extreme was the person who said:

> I never stop thinking about my business. I have no formal hours of work. Quite frankly, I just have a job to do, and my telephone is ringing at home quite constantly. It is an unfortunate part of my life that I am obsessed with my business. Even when 'relaxing' I am thinking about business.

There were others who tried to limit work at home to perhaps an hour in the evening during the week, with usually two or three hours on Sunday preparing for the coming week. All variations between these extremes occurred, some people making a point of trying to keep weekends free to spend unencumbered time with their families. Many felt that their families lost out by their absence during the week, and so tried to compensate in this way.

In addition to these office hours, all of them were involved in considerable travel. One man calculated that during the past year he had travelled 35,000 miles by car and 20,000 miles by train, and had made ten overseas trips outside Europe. Another MD said that he quite frequently left home at 4.00 or 5.00 a.m. to travel to a meeting in some other part of the country, in order to arrive by 9.00 a.m., so as to be able to put in a normal working day.

This lifestyle is well illustrated by the following comments of one of our typical MDs:

> Let me give you this week as an example. I left home [in Manchester] at 5.30 on Monday morning and drove to London for a meeting starting at 9 o'clock. This went on until late afternoon. I then drove to Nottingham to stay overnight *en route* for Yorkshire. I got there at 10.00 p.m. and went to bed, got up at 6.00 and drove to Selby for 8.15. I was there until 7.00 p.m., and then drove back to Manchester [by 8.30]. On Wednesday I was in here [the office] by 8.00 a.m. and left here at 7.30 p.m. On Thursday I got up at 5.00 a.m. and took the shuttle to London for meetings. I got the 8.30 shuttle back at night and got home at about 10 o'clock. This morning I was in here at 8.15. I will probably finish at 6.30.

This was not just an isolated case, or an unusual week. Many of the sample reported this level of activity. A week spent just in the office would be unusual. On top of this, as noted above, most were also making overseas trips several times a year. These ranged from meetings in European cities involving travel the previous evening, meetings during the day and travelling home that evening, to visits to the Far East of one to several weeks' duration.

As a group, they were not strongly interested in holidays. One man admitted: 'I don't like holidays. I only twice ever had more than a week's holiday at a stretch.' Many of them seemed to feel that holidays were something that they owed to their families, rather than something they looked forward to for themselves. There was a minority who enjoyed holidays and looked forward to an annual vacation of usually about two weeks.

Although all this represents a very busy and active life, it did not give the impression of being compulsive or frenetic, except in only one or two cases where individuals admitted to being 'workaholics'. Rather, the general impression is one of people who are very active, enjoy what they are doing and are very involved in their work, in a positive and healthy way.

Work and Motivation

Hence the long work hours and heavy schedule of travel are accepted as a necessary part of life. There were some expressions of guilt that perhaps they did not spend enough time with their families and, particularly, that this lifestyle had placed an undue burden of responsibilty on their wives, for maintenance of the home and for bringing up the children. This issue is discussed in more detail in another section at the end of this chapter.

Patterns of Motivation

One obvious area of interest is what provides the *drive* to reach the top, what motivates managing directors to work the long hours that they do. Accordingly, we asked them about their motivation, drive and ambitions.

Interest and Involvement

The key motivation for our sample was undoubtedly enjoyment of and involvement in the job. Almost universally, when asked what motivated them and kept them working for long hours, the answer was simply 'I enjoy it'. A typical MD response was 'I enjoy working. I love my work. I am not besotted by it, but I enjoy working. I never look at the time. There is never a dull moment.' Often, work is the only real interest in the individual's life, amounting almost to an obsession, as this CEO indicated:

> I am not a workaholic in the sense of working all the hours that God sends, because I don't. I can switch off fairly easily, but I don't care much about anything else. I suppose I am married to the job. I really love the job. I suppose I devote 96 per cent of my energies to it. When I am not here at the job I just watch TV or listen to music.

An even more extreme example is provided by the person who is prepared to subjugate his personal life almost totally to the needs of the organization.

> I was the guy who was always prepared to get on an aeroplane at the drop of a hat – no problem. If it was 'Go to Iran and get an order', it would be OK, to hell with the family, let's go to Iran and get an order.

The motivation is almost entirely intrinsic. Many people mentioned that they liked the trappings which went with the senior position, and the accompanying income which enabled them to live in a style which they and their families enjoyed, but this was a secondary consideration. Some said that money had been a more important factor early in their careers, but that later it was of relatively low importance, in the sense that they now had enough for their needs, and the possibility of a higher income would not affect their actions.

> Another thing I value is working in a business I have always found interesting. Over the years I have never been bored or frustrated. I've always had a job I enjoyed and found interesting and fascinating, to the point that salary has always been a secondary consideration . . . . It's also doing something that has benefits to the community.

Achievement

Achieving targets and objectives was second only to pure 'intrinsic interest' as a motivator. Mostly these achievements were to do with longer-term company development and growth, but sometimes they were also concerned with shorter-term production objectives or product development, as this recent MD suggested:

> I get most satisfaction from developing new products – going to see a customer, identifying a need, coming back and discussing with the designer and the technical people how to fulfil that need, coming up with the product, getting the colours right, seeing it through to the customer and actually seeing it in the market-place. That's still the most satisfying thing I do.

Work and Motivation

The trouble is the further up the ladder you get the less easy it is to spend time doing that.

In other cases, motivation was to do with 'setting targets' and being able to see that they will be achieved.

> The pleasure comes from going home at the end of the week and being able to relax for a few hours, and say: Well now, that is secure, at least I can see my way to doing what I have predicted I am going to do for at least the six months ahead and for this year, possibly.

Ambition

Another factor which seems to have been important in the careers of the managing directors is ambition. This takes a number of forms. Sometimes it is simply a personal drive to suceed, as illustrated by this CEO:

> There's always been an inner drive in me – an ambition to get to whatever the next point on the scale is. I've always felt that I was capable of doing my boss's job. It's just been an inner motivation all my life – in any job, after a year or two, I always felt I had mastered it and was ready to move on to something bigger . . . . There's always a satisfaction in living a little dangerously – extending myself – responding to a challenge.

Sometimes this ambition is directed more towards the overall success of the organization, as another MD suggested:

> I have a burning ambition to be successful. I consider I am not successful at the moment. Given that I am in a difficult trade, this factory is a marvellous factory in every way – minute labour turnover, and it makes a lot of money. 7 per cent net in our business is marvellous. This factory makes an average of 6–10 per cent year after year. Where I have failed is that I cannot repeat that success in the other factories. So my ambition drives me forward. I must be successful.

High Flyers

Determination

The above are all manifestations of a general determination to succeed, which was very strongly expressed by one top executive:

> I'll tell you why I think I have been successful. If my boss sets me an objective and I agree to it, I achieve it against the time scale he sets me. If it means working night and day to achieve it, so be it, but I achieve the objective. I lay heavy stress on this and it has always been a characteristic of me.

Another expression of a similar determination ran as follows:

> I've always felt that I have to struggle slightly to do the job that I'm doing. I think that has been important. I have always wanted to have a job that I can't quite do easily. I think when I can do it easily I tend to lose interest in it. My advice would always be, if you want to get satisfaction from what you do, always do something you can't quite achieve. I've never ever felt so much on top of a job that I can sit with my feet up on the desk and do it in half an hour a day.

Developing the Business

Closely related to the 'personal ambition' and 'drive for success' is the desire, expressed by many of the group, to improve and develop the organization, leaving it better and stronger than they found it. This is the organizational equivalent of 'individual mortality' expressed by many parents when referring to their offspring. The combination of personal and organizational success was clearly expressed by one MD:

> I want to be thought of as a success. This has always been true. When I swotted at school it was not because I wanted to swot, but because I wanted to become top, or near it. I liked to be a success and was prepared to work for it . . . .
>
> I want to be successful personally and I want the company to be a success. I want it to go on after my time – to go on indefinitely.

Work and Motivation

The balance of business success and 'personal extrinsic reward' was described by another. This was a man who had overseen the development of the company, from a relatively small family concern to a large public corporation:

> The aspiration to make the business bigger and better – at my stage of life, to make it better rather than bigger. I derive satisfaction from seeing things running well. I would be stupid to ignore the peripheral, but important, effects of money and social attainment and enjoyment from business life, because I am quite a gregarious guy and it is nice to be invited to dinners and private boxes at sporting events, but these things are peripheral . . . . I suppose what motivates me most is beating last year's profit figures.

The managing director of a very large public company described it as follows:

> It is tremendously exciting to have changed a company from one which in 1981–2 lost £200 million, to one that this year [1986] will make a great deal more than £100 million. That has to be pretty exciting. It was achieved through major restructuring – it has taken up an enormous amount of time, but was worthwhile . . . .
> This is an exciting industry to be in – highly innovative, and the technology is fun.

Working with People

Another important motivator is working with people. Most of those interviewed enjoyed the fact that most of their time was spent working with others. Although most of them had started their careers as specialists (in the main as either accountants or engineers; see chapter 2), very few expressed any great regret at no longer being closely involved with their original technical specialism. In general, they seem to have made the transition to general manager without difficulty, quite possibly because their underlying predispositions were with 'people management'. The combined pleasure of seeing company success and achieving it through people was described by one MD in the following terms:

> The success of the business is important to me – seeing it doing well; seeing the challenges and trying to overcome them; working with people; getting people working as a team, and that's not always easy. You do get times when things are going badly and people are getting fed up with other people, and to keep the team going then is very important and very satisfying.

Another person expressed this more simply and straightforwardly: 'I like achieving things through people – it's what the management process is about.'

Creative Discontent

The urge to improve and develop the business may be part of a deeper personal need to be constantly 'challenging' and 'developing'. Two MDs independently referred to this as 'creative discontent', but the syndrome was mentioned by others. It refers to a general restlessness and discontent with the world as it is, but which takes expression in positive attempts to do something about it:

> There are two main factors in my motivation. One is restlessness. I have only one favourite Americanism – I normally loathe them. My favourite one is 'creative discontent'. I'm very restless, restless to expand, restless to improve, restless to change. The other is a very strong motive – it is to leave the company stronger than when I came to it.

Or, as it was stated alternatively:

> Somehow or other you can't leave things alone. You can't stop saying, 'This could be done better.' You are perpetually self-critical, not only about your own performance, but about the things you see going on. You are never entirely happy with what's going on.

Work and Motivation

Power and Influence

A smaller number of our sample obviously enjoyed the level of control and influence that their position enabled them to exert. This did not seem in any way to be related to possessing or being in a position of exercising power over *people*, but was more to do with influencing events. They tended to speak of the pleasure they felt from knowing that they were in a position to influence the company's success. This is close to the motive of developing the business, discussed above, but has in addition this extra dimension of enjoying the ability to influence – as one CEO put it:

> I like to feel that I am part of the power structure. I don't think I am power hungry, but I like to feel that my voice is heard. I like to feel that I am contributing to running a successful business.

Other chief executives felt it more as a responsibility, and a small minority admitted to enjoying the political aspects of their job:

> I enjoy the responsibility. I enjoy being the person, for example, who is responsible for bringing about a particular contract, or developing a new service. I also quite enjoy the politics of getting something done out of an extremely tangled set of threads and to come to a result which is of best benefit to all the participants – not just to screw the other side.

It is possible that more of the sample actually enjoyed the political aspects of their job than were prepared to admit. There is a strong negative feeling about politics in organizations. Many times, any involvement in political activity was strongly denied, it being seen as divisive and detrimental to the organization. Those who did talk about politics saw it in the more positive light of the above quotation – a matter of balancing the opposing forces which inevitably exist within and outside the organization. This was often related to an ability and enjoyment in negotiating.

Independence

A final theme that emerged concerning motivation was a desire for *independence*. This was mentioned by only a small minority and is probably more to do with control than true independence, which it seems is hard to acquire fully even at the top of a major corporation. As such, it may simply be another manifestation of the need for influence, already discussed.

> Originally to get more independence. I hate people telling me what to do, so it was to reduce the number of people who had authority over me. I don't like to be told what to do . . . .
> It was not power or money . . . .
> Now I think that the thing I am happiest doing is working. I enjoy it. I enjoy the excitement and challenge.

A final quotation will summarize this and all the other themes. There is a slight difference in background, since the MD involved was the fifth generation to manage a still basically family-owned company. Although considerably smaller than the other companies included in the sample, it is a very successful organization, and the MD himself showed many characteristics in common with the rest of the sample. He may, however, have more actual independence than the others.

> To me, business is life. Business is a very wide variety of experience, of situations, of people in all aspects. It has appealed to me because I have found it to be an interesting occupation and a very varied occupation. I suppose, also, I like the responsibility. I like being my own master. One thing I value increasingly is the independence which running a private business gives one, not only in the obvious way that one is not going to be subject to external factors like the stock exchange, takeovers, etc., but also because it gives one confidence in one's independence of mind . . . .
> I look upon life very much as a whole. I don't look at business as something apart. That is not to say, though, that I am obsessed with it, or that I think about it all the time . . . .
> I feel that I am doing something worthwhile.

WORK AND MOTIVATION

MOTIVATION FOR SUCCESS

It seems, then, a common pattern that managing directors of major organizations work very long hours and, very clearly, find this enjoyable. Garfield, in his study of peak performers, sums up this attitude as follows:

> Often they comment that they feel most alive when engaged full throttle. Call it a positive addiction, a contributory obsession, a passion to create one's self through one's work. When asked, 'Why are you so thoroughly involved in your work?', they most frequently answer, 'Because I love it'. To refuse the call, or to diminish the involvement, feels to them like taking a wrong turn, like 'losing one's life in living it'.
> These people are not job addicts or workaholics. A peak performer expresses satisfaction and fulfilment; a job addict, numbness and depletion born of a psychological hunger that cannot be gratified. Rather than using himself fully, the job addict uses himself up. This depletion results from a grinding addiction to activity, which is quite different from a focus on activity with purpose and clear direction.

The motivation for this hard work is almost entirely 'intrinsic'. While most MDs clearly enjoyed the money and status of their position, they all maintained that this was quite secondary to the other motives. This applied, at any rate, in their present situation. For some of them, financial motivation was more important in the early stages of their careers. In some cases, this may have been linked to a need to escape from early poverty (see chapter 2, on 'Childhood events'). G. Copeman, in *The Chief Executive and Business Growth*, found almost the same pattern of motivation that we did. According to his summary,

> Some 15% of the chief executives in the survey seem to be primarily motivated by enjoyment of their work. Next in order of importance amongst the motivators mentioned were a desire to prove himself, an urge to create something new, and a

striving for perfection. These together make up almost half the primary explanations of personal motivation. Only after these comes the desire for more money. It must, however, be noted that chief executives have already arrived at the top and, except in some cases in Britain, those included in the survey were certainly not short of money.

This is a pattern which also emerges in other studies of successful people. Mumford (in Mumford, Robinson and Stradling, *Developing Directors*) found that the main motivation of directors was not financial, but to do their present job well. Cooper and Hingley's survey of *The Change Makers* and Leah Hertz's study of women entrepreneurs, *The Business Amazons*, both found a similar pattern of high energy and high involvement with the job, with little reported concern for extrinsic motivators. This may well be because they *are* high achievers. As D. C. McClelland has pointed out in his article 'Achievement motivation can be developed':

> It is people with low achievement need who require money incentives to make them work harder. The person with a high need [of achievement] works hard anyway, providing there is an opportunity of achieving something. He is interested in money rewards or profits primarily because of the feedback they give him as to how well he is doing.

This orientation is consistent with McClelland's 'leadership motivation pattern' (*Power: The Inner Experience*). This is a pattern of at least moderately high need for power, with a lower need for affiliation (or need to be liked), and high self-control. It is important that the need for power is expressed in terms of influencing people to achieve organizational ends; it is not personal power over others for its own sake. McClelland and Boyatzis demonstrated that managers showing the leadership motivation pattern achieved higher levels of management advancement in non-technical jobs.

The MDs in our study showed a fairly high need for institutionalized power in their concern for developing the organization, but achieving it through people. Their need for

McClelland's socio-motivational drives

McClelland identified three important motivational drives

Need for Achievement (N Ach)
Need for Power (N Pow)
Need for Affiliation (N Aff)

Need for Achievement

People with a high level of N Ach need to feel a sense of achievement and so prefer situations where they have direct control over their success or failure and in which they can obtain immediate feedback on how well they are doing. They tend to take moderate and calculated risks and prefer working on their own. Managers who are high on N Ach tend to be individualists and to avoid holding meetings, even though the problems they are dealing with might be better solved by collaborative effort. Because of the constraints imposed by the organization, a high Need for Achievement can be dysfunctional for a manager unless moderated by other considerations. It is a vital characteristic for the entrepreneur.

Need for Power

N Pow is a need to gain control over and receive recognition from others. Most managers show reasonably high levels of this need. High N Pow on its own can lead to excessively authoritarian managerial styles which are not generally effective. Need for Power seems to be a necessary but not sufficient condition for successful management.

Need for Affiliation

The individual with a high Need for Affiliation is concerned to maintain warm and friendly relationships. A manager who is high on N Aff will be concerned to maintain good relationships, possibly at the expense of task performance unless again this need is balanced by other factors. Research indicates that N Aff may be present but is seldom dominant in successful people.

affiliation (in the organizational setting) seems relatively low. This is probably what some of them meant by 'independence'. Their relative detachment from people was also shown in a number of accounts of having to make employees redundant. While this was clearly a painful experience, they were able to avoid close empathy with the feelings of those who were sacked. This is undoubtedly a necessary skill, rather like the professional detachment of a doctor carrying out an operation. It was nearly always explained in terms of sacrificing the minority for the good of the majority, by maintaining the viability of the company as a whole and thus safeguarding other jobs. Virtually everyone placed a very high value on family life and the need for a supportive wife (see chapter 5), and it was in this context that their affiliation needs were met.

It is interesting that McClelland and Boyatzis also found that more junior managers showed higher levels of need for achievement than the more senior. They explained this by the suggestion that promotion at the lower levels depends more on individual contribution. McClelland's concept of 'need for achievement' is, of course, concerned with very direct personal achievement. Since the chief executives in our sample also talked of achievement, it seems to us that what may happen is that, as a manager rises through an organization, he still maintains a need to achieve, but measures this increasingly in terms of organizational objectives. Certainly our sample seemed to consider the way in which their organizations had developed to be very much a reflection of their own achievement, even though, of course, many others had also been involved.

Life Outside Work

Since managing directors work so hard, it is interesting to know whether, in compensation, they also 'play hard'. In general they do not seem to . In fact, their very busy lives leave little time for 'out of work' activities. In most cases what spare time they have is spent with the family and in 'pottering' in the house and garden. Those who mentioned other spare-time activities were mainly involved in physically active pastimes, the most popular being golf, walking, fishing (exclusively game fishing for trout and salmon) and shooting. These are obviously enjoyed for their own sake, but also for the health value of the exercise. There is a notable lack of intellectual pastimes, with only a few MDs mentioning reading, listening to music and attending concerts and the theatre. One played jazz on the piano, finding that an hour of hammering out jazz themes was a good way to unwind after a hard day.

The Importance of a Supportive Wife and Family

One theme that was absolutely universal was the importance of a supportive wife and family. One of the questions we asked was 'Have you found there to be much conflict between work and family life?' The answer to this was usually 'no', since wives had been prepared to cope with the family and household problems, leaving their husbands free to concentrate on work and their careers. These wives in general did not have careers of their own. Many MDs paid tribute to the sacrifices which their wives had made in this way. Marriages were thus very stable; only three MDs had been divorced. Much of this pattern is, without doubt, a function of the age of this group. It is likely that the next generation of MDs will have to find a way of coping with dual-career families. It is significant that the divorcees were from the younger end of the age range and the youngest of them did admit that his divorce was caused by his commitment to work. This view is summarized by the comments of one chief executive:

> I believe I was fortunate in not having a career-oriented wife. My generation is fortunate in having wives who saw it as their job to support their husbands in their careers. The conflict seems to come where you have a wife with ambitions of her own, which she cannot fulfil because of family commitments, and therefore she is turning to her husband and saying, 'Hang on, you ought to be sharing some of these family commitments.'

... There is a noticeably higher divorce or separation rate with my younger colleagues.

He did, however, see some reciprocity in the relationship, in that he added: 'I have also devoted most of my spare time to the family.' Another MD took a much more extreme view:

> I don't believe you can succeed with a 90 per cent effort. I think you need an understanding wife, who does not care that you don't phone in and say when you are going to be home; a wife who does not care when you say, 'I am going to be off to South Africa next week', or 'I am going to Germany tomorrow' – who just takes it in her stride. If you have got to be looking over your shoulder all the time wondering what impact it is having on her, then I think you will find it very difficult to succeed. I have seen evidence of this. I have seen people puzzled as to why they are failing and I can see quite clearly, it is when they are only able to give 90 per cent dedication because of 'What will the wife think?' or 'I had better have a day off because it is a while since I saw her.'

Another chief executive appreciated the support of a stable home life as a background to, and refuge from, the pressures of his daily work life:

> I think at this level it can be a lonely job, because at the end of the day it's you who have to make the decisions. You can talk to colleagues and get their views, but in the end you have to make your mind up and get on with it. That can be lonely in some ways – the buck stops here as it were – and I think having support from one's wife and a stable home is important.

It should be recorded that there were one or two examples of two-career families, where the wife also had a demanding job, and these marriages also seemed to work very well. It is significant that they were also among the younger members of the group and were very much the exception to the rule.

This pattern of stable marriage and home background is supported by other studies. D. Norburn, in a study of corporate leaders in Britain and America, found that

Top managers in both countries experienced very little domestic trauma in terms of parental divorce or of their own, the rate being less than one-third of the two national averages. Where marital trauma was experienced, that of the US manager emanated from spouse morbidity, whereas the UK manager was more likely to be divorced or separated.

G. Kushel, in a study of 550 American top executives, *The 4%*, found that only 4 per cent were what he called *fully effective executives* (FEEs): 'These highly effective executives not only had success in their jobs, with salaries ranging from 58 to 325 thousand dollars a year, but they also enjoyed their work very much. In addition, they had excellent personal lives which complemented their success at work.' Their attitude to marriage, however, as described by Kushel, does seem a little different from that shown by the MDs in our study.

> FEEs look upon being married, at least in part, as 'living alone together with someone very special'. Their version of marriage is of two separate, whole individuals combining their unique resources into a winning team. The formula, then, for marriage is not the usual one half person plus another half person equals one whole marriage ($\frac{1}{2} + \frac{1}{2} = 1$ marriage). Instead, FEEs view marriage as one whole person plus one additional whole person plus one marriage, which adds up to three (1 person + 1 person + 1 marriage = 3). If a person has his or her act together and then joins another in marriage, prospects of a successful marriage are much greater. And those FEEs who married knew how to make their marriages work.

What is being described here is what we would call an *interdependent* marriage, where each partner is an independent individual capable of interacting in many different roles with 'the other'. It is particularly characterized by the partners' ability to interchange roles. We suspect that the few younger MDs in our sample with successful marriages in which the wife had a career of her own, did operate in this way, and that this is probably the pattern for the future. It can be a very supportive and satisfying relationship, but requires a great deal of energy to keep it going.

The majority of the MDs we interviewed were clearly in a relationship characterized by *mutual dependence*. This is where each partner has a very clear and separate role which they do not interchange – in this case, with the wife looking after the home and family while the husband provides for them by earning the income (the traditional homemaker/hunter dichotomy). This can also be very powerful and supportive, but is also felt to be constraining by each of the partners. The wife feels that she cannot develop outside the home, and the husband feels he must look after her. This was demonstrated by comments that wives occasionally became angry at their husband's neglect of them because of his involvement in his work, and many MDs themselves expressed guilt at this state of affairs. As many of the MDs recognized, mutually dependent marriages were very much the norm for their generation, but, with the increasing demand by women to have lives outside the home, marriages, even for top executives, will have to move towards interdependence. The signs are that this is happening.

Summary

The motivation of successful managing directors springs from their being ambitious and determined people with a reasonably high need of achievement, who find managing a major company an interesting, enjoyable and worthwhile activity. They have a restlessness and feeling of discontent with their current situation, which is expressed, not in complaints about the situation, but in a drive to do something about it; hence their pleasure in developing the business and its products. They also enjoy working with people, have some need of power, and also require some degree of independence. Perhaps this was best summed up by William James, one of America's most eminent psychologists, as long ago as 1906:

> Most people live, whether physically, intellectually or morally, in a very restricted circle of their potential being. They make

use of a very small portion of their possible consciousness, of their soul's resources in general, much like a man who, out of his whole bodily organism, should get into the habit of using and moving only his little finger. Great emergencies and crises show us how much greater our vital resources are than we had supposed.

Perhaps successful MDs and other high achievers have managed to release a little more of these 'vital resources' than the average, but it must be remembered that in order for an individual to achieve self-actualization he must engage in *work* which offers the opportunity for growth and development, as well as the necessary personal potential. As was discussed in chapter 3, there seems to be an element of luck in whether this opportunity does occur at the appropriate time in a person's career, and this has implications for management development programmes.

5
VALUES

Everything that we do is influenced by our values – how we run our lives, our ambitions, how we relate to others. A value may be defined as an enduring belief, a specific way of behaving or 'of being', which is preferable to any other. We usually have a complex set of interrelated values in each aspect of our life, and this is known as a *value system*. Frequently, this system of beliefs may be all-embracing and complex enough to guide our whole life, as in a religious system.

In relation to managers, England and Lee make the following assertions:

1 Personal value systems influence a manager's perception of situations and problems he faces.
2 Personal value systems influence a manager's decisions and solutions to problems.
3 Personal value systems influence the way in which a manager looks at other individuals and groups of individuals; thus they influence interpersonal relationships.
4 Personal value systems influence the perception of individual and organizational success as well as their achievement.
5 Personal value systems set the limits for the determination of what is and what is not ethical behaviour by a manager.

Values

6   Personal value systems influence the extent to which a manager accepts or resists organizational pressures and goals.
7   Some personal value systems may contribute to managerial performance, some may be irrelevant, and some may be antithetical to achievement efforts.

Two areas in which a chief executive's values are particularly significant are those of decision-making, including the definition of objectives, and the influence he has on the culture of the organization. This, in turn, will influence the way in which people are treated in the organization and how they relate to each other. The point is made in the following quotation from Cooper and Hingley's *The Change Makers*:

> Sir Peter Parker (then Chairman of British Rail) made a point of stressing the importance of a well worked out system of values as a guide to effective decision making. Quoting Johnson's comment that 'nothing so much needs a philosophy than business', he stressed that managerial action must be grounded in a well developed philosophy of action, of cause and effect. In his view a clearly thought out idea of purpose and values together with professional skills and abilities were the hallmarks of the successful manager.

In *The New Competitors*, D. Q. Mills draws attention to the fact that, in the past, what he calls 'the American work ethic' – an all-embracing value system – was a major influence on American commercial success: 'Years ago the churches, immigrant groups, and the media promoted attitudes favouring hard work, commitment, risk taking, savings and deferred gratification. The American work ethic was alive and well. Corporations drew from the society employees already imbued with attitudes favourable to competitive business.' He goes on to point out that nowadays, with the decline of the work ethic as a value in society, companies have to develop it as part of their internal culture. Using the example of Japanese companies, he observes:

The decline of the American work ethic is especially evident to managers coming to this country from places where the work ethic is alive and well. To Japanese and Korean managers, for example, the work values of rank and file Americans seem shortsighted, greedy and unproductive. To them, if a company is going to be successful with an American work force, it must spend considerable time and effort developing a more constructive set of work attitudes.

Identical comments could be made concerning Britain during the early part of this century and at the present time. It should be stressed that the use of the above quotations is not intended to endorse the work ethic. We are using them simply as examples of the interrelation between values and culture – in this case, both national and organizational. In terms of a discussion of managerial values, it is obviously important for us to remain neutral, although, because of the all-pervading influence of values, this is all but impossible to do.

Exploring Managerial Values

Since values have so much influence on our actions, some exploration of this area is essential if we are to gain greater understanding of the successful managing director. We did this by means of three questions. First, we simply asked our respondents what their values were and what they valued in life. We then asked what advice they would give to a son or daughter about how to be successful in life, and what they would like to see as their epitaph; these two questions should reveal underlying values. Interestingly the 'advice question' produced some quite rich data, but most respondents had difficulty with the epitaph. It was as if they were unwilling, or unable, to contemplate such a situation, possibly because they were all very action-oriented and highly involved in 'living'.

VALUES

Family

The theme which came through most strongly was a very high value placed on the family and family life. Many MDs commented that their lives would be quite impossible without a supportive wife and a stable home life. Having this made it possible to concentrate on work, as one MD commented:

> A stable and happy home life is essential – and a supportive wife. You can then take the time to run the business, if you've got a patient and understanding wife . . . .
> I am also very committed. If a job is worth doing, do it well. I don't take on something I am not committed to. If you can't do it properly, don't do it.

For others it was much more the family for its own sake, as two senior chief executives suggested:

> My family is the most important thing in my life.

> I have always put the welfare of my family first and foremost, and I don't mean just material welfare . . . the company comes a long second after that.

There was, however, a small minority for whom the job took precedence, with the family, for the most part, coming second, as illustrated here:

> My job is my life. I think I have to say that my job is number one and my family is number two, unless it came to a real crisis in the family. Then, of course, it would have to be number one, but in the ordinary day to day, year in, year out, I'm afraid I put my job in front of my family.

People and Relationships

Another large group of expressed 'values' were concerned with *respect for other people*, as a recent MD reflected:

You've got to start with that recognition of people. If you don't start with people, then really, in my opinion, you don't start with anything. There's got to be a consideration – a recognition of people. You have to start with a concern and a feeling for people .... You must have compassion and consideration in implementing your decisions.

Another MD expressed this in terms of being honest with people:

> I think the value I would espouse and try to live by is: 'Be honest with people.' First check if they want the honesty, and if they want it give it to them. People can deal with the truth – they can't deal with uncertainty, although some people can only deal with uncertainty because they don't want the truth.

For some chief executives, the important thing was to keep a balance between relationships and work:

> Personal relationships – with family, friends and people I work with – are the most important single thing for me, very much so. I would never want to take business advantage at the expense of a personal relationship .... It is possible that the Quakers had a lot to do with that. [While not a Quaker, he had attended a Quaker school.] They really impressed on me, at an impressionable age, the importance of human values. I am very grateful to them.

One man expressed very clearly this need to keep a balance between the three elements of job, family and others:

> My job is of paramount importance to me. In terms of my wellbeing, without my job, I don't know that much would be worthwhile at all ....
> Equally my family is a great source of joy and comfort ....
> People are important – meeting people, talking with them, learning about their experiences of life.

This same theme was eloquently and enthusiastically expressed by another MD:

Values

I think that life is wonderful; it's to be appreciated every moment. It is necessary to get the three parts of your life in balance – work, your family life, and the most important thing to to take time for yourself. Whether it's one minute a day or an hour a day, or a day a week – whatever it is, you need the time to give you independence from your wife and children and from work. It is your time, where you indulge yourself. For me, it's playing golf – it's the most selfish practice in the world, but I need that time. It has that happy blend of fresh air and physical effort and the challenge of playing better.

Achievement

Since achievement was high on the list of factors motivating managing directors, it is not surprising that it is also something that they value. Achievement and/or ambition was mentioned by many of them, as illustrated by the following chief executive:

> I am ambitious in the sense of doing the current thing well – doing my present job well. I remember being asked this question [about values] twenty years ago, and I can remember saying that if my job was a lavatory cleaner I am sure that I would strive to see that my loo was the cleanest.

This man's advice to his son was: 'Find something you enjoy doing and work hard, but don't be over-ambitious – know your limitations.' Another MD similarly valued achievement:

> I like organizing things, I like achieving, I like seeing results, I like to see progress, I like to see improvements, and therefore, whether it's the football club or business, or whatever it is, I like to say, 'Hang on – let's take a look at what we are doing. Can we improve it?' That seems to be a driving force within me.

One of the few clear responses to a request for an epitaph ran as follows:

> I would like, when I retire, to be able to look back on a career and say, 'I did influence major situations in a positive way and

> *Integration and faith*
> An adequate value system is both internally consistent and integrated with the individual's total personality. It is something in which he can reasonably have good faith. An integrated value system also implies a *hierarchy* of values, which enables the individual to choose confidently between things of greater and lesser importance and to be relatively undisturbed by frustrations that interfere only with the attainment of short-range goals.
> Values come alive in direct proportion to how much faith the individual has in them. Faith helps close the gap between conceived and operative values and enables the individual to achieve a sense of wholeness in everything he feels and says and does. His behaviour reflects an intellectual and emotional surety; there is relatively little conflict between 'ought' and 'want'. This is the kind of faith illustrated in the lives of men whose actions seem in complete harmony with their deepest wishes. Maslow described it as one characteristic of self-actualizing people.
> (J. C. Coleman, *Psychology and Effective Behaviour*, Scott, Foresman and Company, Glenview, 1969)

I have a visible record of achievement', rather than having occupied a position of authority for ten years and not changed anything . . . .

To sum up [I would like to feel that] I have achieved something and made my own and my family's life secure in the process.

Independence and Self-Reliance

As with achievement, *independence* was an important motivator that was also reflected as a 'value':

> If you ask me what is my aim in life, I think it is to be independent, and when I say independent it is not to be beholden to anybody. To be able to act when I want to and not to be constrained by some other influences.

VALUES

This same MD, when asked what advice he would give his son or daughter, said: 'Take a career in which they can determine their own destiny.' This seems to be closely related to a value on *self-reliance*, which figured very strongly in advice to children, such as 'Self-reliance is one of the things I try to get over to my children.' Sometimes this came over as a sort of sturdy independence, as this chief executive suggested:

> You've got to fight and to battle. I don't mean that in a nasty sense, but you've got to work. I think grafting and working and being seen to be pulling your weight is very important. Life does not owe you anything. You've got to work for it and be seen to be working for it. Be a genuine person seen to be pulling his weight.

This is related to an ability to take 'hard decisions', as another MD reported:

> With these enormous organizations you have to have a drive. You have to be harder than you would like inside. You have to be prepared to be insular. I find that the hardest part of being at the top, because very big decisions are yours – like factory closures. I wrestle with those for nights, and I am ashamed to say some of those decisions do keep me awake at nights, although I have a temperament which can usually shrug them off.

Initiative

Showing initiative was mentioned by several people as an important piece of advice to their son or daughter, although no one mentioned it as a characteristic they valued in themselves. One MD coupled this with the need for hard work:

> The first thing is that there is no easy road; it's hard work. You will not get there without that. There is no golden escalator – you've got to work hard. When you go home each night, ask yourself, "Have you displayed initiative during that day?' If you go for two days running with the answer 'No', you'd

better make sure that on the third you do. I used to use that myself, because it's very easy just to go and do the job, but you've got to think beyond that. These are the two key things – work hard and show initiative . . . . If you want to move on you must, partly, create the opportunities.

Another stressed independence as well as the need to do 3 per cent more than the next man:

> I would give two pieces of advice that my father gave to me: (1) Always have enough money in the bank so that you can live without any income at all for six months. Then you can tell any boss to go to hell . . . . (2) Do 3 per cent more than the next bloke. It's not a lot to do, 3 per cent, but it's enough to be obvious. That's a very good piece of advice. I give all my kids that advice.

Being Yourself

Another frequent piece of advice to children was, in effect, to 'be themselves'. This was expressed by one man in terms of Polonius's advice to Laertes, 'To thine own self be true', or in another case, more prosaically: 'Do what you are good at and what you enjoy – usually the two are the same.' Or, as in the case of another senior MD, pointing out that there are other important qualities than academic achievement:

> It is important that everyone be brought up to aspire to do something that they really enjoy doing, and also to aspire to making the best use of the talents they happen to have . . . . We overweigh academic abilities and underweigh other characteristics. I have seen people ahead of me academically, but who somehow failed to take advantage of that . . . . I tell my children that life is not just about academic achievement – there are plenty of opportunities outside that.

For another top manager, this was linked to reliability:

> I have always said to my own kids, 'Be reliable – be seen as someone whom others can trust and believe in. Don't try to

be something that you are not. If you don't understand things, say so. Don't try to bluff.

Integrity

Honesty and integrity were 'values' mentioned either directly or indirectly by many of our MDs. They would emphasize these in describing important personal characteristics, in their advice to others and in their own life goals, as this MD illustrates:

> I value integrity. I have no patience with dishonesty in business. I would like to be thought of as having run an open and honest ship, but successful – needless to say.

Perfection

A desire for perfection was mentioned in only two or three cases; for example:

> I'm a striver for perfection and success in all facets of my life – running a company, my marriage, my family or hobbies.

It may well be that in an area such as managing a large corporation, where there are so many factors outside the manager's control, too much emphasis on a desire for perfection would actually be a negative characteristic. Life in such circumstances must often be a matter of simply doing the best one can.

MANAGERIAL VALUE SYSTEMS

Clare and Sanford, using a distinction made by Rokeach between *terminal* values and *instrumental* values, found little difference in the values of managers at different levels in the organization, but concluded that there was a distinctive set of values subscribed to by most managers. *Terminal values* are

> Clearly any successful top executive must have a given degree of personal drive, the mental equipment required for running the business he or she is running (this will vary with the nature of the business) and the ability to win the co-operation of others. Having said that, what strikes me is the disparity between the characteristics of successful executives whom I have met around the world. The key may lie in that sound piece of Shakespearean advice, now alas a cliché—'to thine own self be true'.
>
> (Sir Adrian Cadbury, Chairman, Cadbury Schweppes plc)

long-range life goals; *instrumental values* concern the appropriate behaviour and methods for achieving these long-term goals. The following list shows the order of the top nine values in each category for American managers.

1 *Terminal values*
   Sense of accomplishment
   Self-respect
   Comfortable life
   Freedom
   Wisdom
   Exciting life
   Social recognition
   World at peace
   Pleasure
2 *Instrumental values*
   Ambition
   Capability
   Logic
   Independence
   Broadmindedness
   Self-control
   Imagination
   Helpfulness
   Cheerfulness

Values

From this it can be seen that the most important terminal values are a 'sense of accomplishment' and 'self-respect', while the two leading instrumental values are 'ambition' and 'capability'. England and Lee, on the other hand, did find differences between successful and less successful managers. Defining success in terms of whether the manager was earning above or below the average for his age, they found that

> successful managers tend to emphasize pragmatic, dynamic, achievement-oriented values, while less successful managers prefer more static and passive values . . . . [Successful managers] value a dynamic environment and are willing to take risks to achieve organizationally valued goals. Relatively less successful managers have values associated with a static, protected environment in which they take relatively passive roles.

Both the above studies found that there were some, but not very significant, differences in managerial values between managers in different companies and different countries, but more importantly that there is considerable consistency in their values and that these are related to success.

A theme which occurs quite frequently in the literature, and was also often mentioned by the managing directors in our study, is that of *integrity*. M. Sorcher regards this as one of the key characteristics to look for in the selection of senior managers. In *Predicting Executive Success* he quotes the policy of Chase Manhattan Bank:

> Integrity is one of the very important personal characteristics Chase seeks in its management. A lack of integrity involves devious behaviour which results in losing the trust of customers, employees and the public. Not surprisingly, candidates who are well qualified in all other respects for senior positions are removed from final candidacy because their peers, subordinates, or managers simply do not trust them. Their intentions and promises are suspect.

Goldsmith and Clutterbuck make a similar point in *The Winning Streak* when talking of successful British companies:

> First of all the most important characteristic in any senior executive is integrity.
>
> How to assess this, of course, is not an easy problem, but one has to study behaviour and performance and family life over a long period of time. In general my experience has been that people who have not exhibited this characteristic usually have deficient performance.
>
> With integrity, of course, goes honesty, and here the assessment will have to be whether a person is not only morally honest but also mentally honest.
>
> Another characteristic that is extremely important in candidates for top responsibilities must be intellectual capacity, including the awareness of all facets of the world in which we live and also a willingness to examine and analyse the possible alternatives to any set of circumstances. This might be described as intellectual curiosity–the exhibition of unwillingness to accept things as they are without a sceptical examination of the other possibilities. Of course, superimposed on all this, it is essential that the person has a clear understanding of the business in which he is involved and, especially today, of the technical world in which we operate.
>
> (Sir Ian MacGregor, former Chairman of British Steel Corporation and the National Coal Board)

'The reaction of these companies to any aspersions on their integrity is swift and vehement. Normally staid and placid chairmen's blood will boil at the suggestion that their company has been dishonest, sharp-practising or deliberately negligent.' They go on to say that integrity is very much part of the culture of these companies, and that this is displayed towards customers, employees, suppliers and the public at large.

This emphasis on integrity does have a very practical orientation. McCall and Lombardo suggest:

> Integrity seems to have a special meaning to executives that is vastly different from it's Mom-and-apple-pie image. The word does not refer to simple honesty, but embodies a consistency and predictability built over time that says, 'I will do exactly what I will say I will do when I say I will do it. If I change

my mind, I will tell you well in advance so you will not be harmed by my actions.' Such a statement is partly one of ethics, but more, it may be one of deadly practicality. This seems to be the core method keeping a large, amorphous organization from collapsing in its own confusion.

McCall and Lombardo also look at the other side of the coin – the effect of 'lack of integrity'. Betrayal of trust comes quite high (third) on the list of reasons why previously successful executives have suddenly failed.

> In an incredibly complex and confusing job, being able to trust others absolutely is a necessity. Some committed what is perhaps management's only unforgivable sin – they betrayed a trust. This rarely had anything to do with honesty (which was a given in almost all cases), rather it was a one-upping of others or a failure to follow through on promises, which wreaked havoc on organizational efficiency.

The popular stereotype, also portrayed in popular literature, of the big-business executive wheeling and dealing seems to be far from reality. Even investigators of business success can perpetuate the myth. Leah Hertz, in her study of female entrepreneurs, whom she calls *Business Amazons* in an analogy with Greek mythology, also noted that they rate 'integrity' very highly: 'Some women magnates even went so far as to suggest that without integrity one could not succeed.' She goes on to argue: 'It is doubtful whether male entrepreneurs of the business Amazon's calibre would attribute their success or any part of it to integrity.' The data show otherwise. Is this, perhaps, a touch of female chauvinism showing through.

Another theme in the value system of our managing directors was the *valuing of people*. This is closely related to integrity and is also a central value in Hopson and Scally's concept (in *Lifeskills Teaching*) of the 'self-empowered person': 'The self-empowered person, by our definition, has values which include recognizing the worth of self and others, of being proactive, working for health systems, at home, in employment, in the community and at leisure; helping other people to become more self-empowered.' This is totally consistent with the values expressed by our respondents, whom we would certainly see as 'self-empowered'.

It is, perhaps, also worth noting the overlap of the above values with the listing by Peters and Waterman in *In Search of Excellence* of the values to be found within successful companies:

1 A belief in being the 'best'
2 A belief in the importance of the details of execution, the nuts and bolts of doing the job well
3 A belief in the importance of people as individuals
4 A belief in superior quality and service
5 A belief that most members of the organization should be innovators, and its corollary, the willingness to support failure
6 A belief in the importance of informality to enhance communication
7 Explicit belief in and recognition of the importance of economic growth and profits.

The only one not explicitly mentioned by our Managing Directors is the final one, concerning economic growth and profits. From our interviews, in general, there can be no doubt that they do subscribe to this one. That they did not mention it as a specific value is due to the fact that our interviews were concentrating on personal rather than organizational matters.

Interestingly, there was not much mention of religion. Some MDs did refer to Christian beliefs, but this was usually in terms of a general system of ethics rather than a close involvement with the church. Very few mentioned actual membership of and attendance at church as being important in their lives. This is consistent with the findings of England and Lee that religion was either uncorrelated or correlated negatively with managerial success. By contrast, many of Cooper and Hingley's 'change makers' did refer to strong Christian convictions. All the values expressed by our MDs were totally consistent with Christian ethics, but this is not

VALUES

particularly surprising, given the culture within which the study took place.

SUMMARY

The values of the chief executives in this survey are centred very strongly around a *valuing of people and relationships*, the central relationships being within the family, with working relationships coming a close second. Many of them stress the need to keep a balance between the demands of work and family, and their personal needs. Much of this relates to the very high value placed on 'integrity'. Closely following, in importance, was a value on achievement and ambition, which fits the motivational pattern discussed in chapter 4. A third group of values is concerned with 'independence and self-reliance'.

One final point which emerged from the section of our interviews on motivation and values is that all the MDs were very proactive, and placed a high value on being involved in life and ready to take opportunities as they arose. This was well expressed by one MD as follows:

> I have an old friend whom I fish with. After about an hour he sits on the bank and puts his rod down, and he lights his pipe. Then he potters up to talk to me and then I catch the fish and he gets furious. I say to him, 'You don't catch fish without having your rod in the water', and I am sure that's true of life. You've got to be out taking an interest in what's going on. I've always tried to do that.

6
MANAGERIAL SKILLS

It is perhaps surprising, but very little is known, even now, about what managers actually do. That is to say, there is not a great deal of recorded information about the detailed day-to-day activities and behaviour of managers. One of the earliest studies by Rosemary Stewart, *Managers and their Jobs* (1967), established that they spent the greater proportion of their time in interaction with other people (see table 6.1). In *The Chief Executive and Business Growth* (1971), G. Copeman also found that chief executives spent over 70 per cent of their time with others, mainly in meetings of various kinds. One by-product of this was that they had to do most of their personal work – reading and writing reports, planning, and so on – in their 'own time', that is, out of normal working hours. Although no one mentioned it, this would imply that skill in rapid reading would be important; perhaps this is taken for granted.

A more recent study designed to throw light on the activities of chief executives is *The Nature of Managerial Work* (1973) by H. H. Mintzberg, who recorded in detail the activities during one week of five CEOs from a range of different types of organization. From an analysis of these data, he suggested that there are six important characteristics of managerial work:

1 Managers do a great deal of work at an unrelenting pace.
2 Management activity is characterized by variety and fragmentation.

MANAGERIAL SKILLS

TABLE 6.1   Average proportion of managers' time spent on various activities

Activities	Percentage
Informal discussions	43
Paperwork	36
Committees	7
Telephone	6
Inspection of others	6
Social activities	4

Source: R. Stewart, *Managers amd their Jobs*, Macmillan, London, 1967

3 Managers prefer dealing with current issues which are specific, and tend to do this in an *ad hoc* way.
4 The manager is at the interface of a network of contacts.
5 Managers have a strong preference for verbal communication.
6 The manager appears to be in control of his own affairs, despite the range of demands made on him.

He also defined ten managerial roles, as listed below.

Interpersonal roles
1 Figurehead and symbol
2 Leader defining group's ethos
3 Liaison with other leaders

Informational roles
4 Monitor of information
5 Disseminator of information
6 Spokesman to others outside group

Decision-making roles
7 Entrepreneur
8 Disturbance-handler and trouble-shooter
9 Resource allocator

Negotiating role
10 Negotiator

Three of these are concerned with interpersonal activities, three with providing information and three with decision-making; the tenth role is as a 'negotiator'. All this would imply that both interpersonal and decision-making skills are vitally important.

Using a multinational sample of chief executives, Copeman found them to need five key skills:

1 *Numerical skills* – facility with arithmetic operations but not higher mathematics.
2 *System skills* – the ability to design and operate business systems, e.g. ordering, accountancy, production control, etc.
3 *Social skills* – the ability to get things done through a significant number of other people. (The word 'significant' is important because operating through a large organization is a different order of skill from working through just one or two people.)
4 *Negotiating skills* – the ability to make a successful agreement with a free and independent person not in a subordinate role.
5 *Policy-making skills* – concerned with knowing where the business is going rather than how to get there.

More recently, in a study of British directors, *Developing Directors*, Mumford, Robinson and Stradling listed the following as the skills reported during their interviews:

identifying strategic direction;
taking a corporate view, rather than representing a function or division;
absorbing and recalling quantities of data without losing sight of main issues;
planning the future more than managing the present;

managing external relationships;
operating effectively in different organizational and national cultures;
influencing directors as powerful as yourself;
getting others to act rather than doing it yourself;
maintaining relationships with non-executive directors.

While there is considerable overlap in all these studies, concerning both what top managers do and the skills that they need to do it, one interesting feature is that very little mention is made of *leadership*. A similar point is made by Goldsmith and Clutterbuck in their study of successful British companies, *The Winning Streak*: 'few of the most successful companies make a song and dance about leadership, yet in all of them managers down the line pinpoint effective leadership at chairman or chief executive level as a key to their own motivation and the companies success.' The chief executive is, obviously, a key figure in the organization, and the leadership and managerial skills which he brings to the job will be of fundamental importance.

The Skills of the Chief Executive

With this in mind, we asked our chief executives what they considered to be their *key skills*. Interestingly, leadership was not often mentioned. the key skill which was mentioned by virtually everyone in the sample was concerned with 'analytical and decision-making abilities'.

Analysis and Problem-Solving

There are a number of different aspects to this skill. At root it is an ability to dissect a problem in a logical and scientific way, as one senior MD suggested:

> [My key skill is] logical analysis, which stems from my engineering background: trying to strip a problem down to its

absolute essentials. Despite what's happening in the information-analysis field, I believe that one of the skills [for an MD] is to do clean, elegant analysis, but be prepared to take the decision on what will always be inadequate information.

Even this very scientific approach recognizes that the information available will always be inadequate; thus decisions will always be, to some extent, intuitive. The next quotation, while reinforcing the above, leads us to another important aspect of decision-making, as seen by many of our managing directors, and illustrated by a more seasoned MD:

> Analysis ability – I try to consider all the aspects, consider various points of view and distil a course of action, and then stick to it. This is both logical and intuitive. The follow-through is also important.

This is the ability, having analysed a problem and decided what should be done, actually to put the decision into effect:

> Having carried out the analysis and taken the decision, the next thing, I would say, is a very clear determination to both make that solution work and to reappraise it, at whatever are appropriate intervals, particularly to make sure the assumptions which formed part of the original decisions are still valid, or, for that matter, the facts on which the decision is based are still valid. Then, not to be afraid to change direction if the review suggests that is necessary.

This was sometimes extended into an ability to make unpleasant decisions, as this chief executive explains:

> I have no hesitation in taking unpleasant decisions, if I think it is the right decision. It is important to make decisions – you will be forgiven for the occasional bad decision, but you must make decisions.

This skill relates to both determination and the ability to be detached from the consequences of unpleasant decisions (e.g. redundancies and factory closures), which was discussed as an

Managerial Skills

> *The importance of analytical and policy-making skills*
>
> The work of a chief executive in forming business policy, with the help of his colleagues and staff, may be likened to the position of a man in a well-lit room peering out into the darkness of night. Everything in the room is visible and real and can be trusted. The inside of the well-lit room is analogous to the inside of his firm. He has buildings and employees and equipment, stocks and accounts, etc. These are real enough, even if occasionally some of the people seem enigmatic in their behaviour. But they at least have definable roles.
>
> By contrast, as a business policy-maker he has to peer into the outer darkness. Somewhere out there are his customers. They are never so real, however much market research he does to help him understand them. He can up to a point measure their spending power, their needs and attitudes and various other characteristics, but when it comes to launching a new product or service, or opening a new branch, he doesn't really know in advance whether and how much they are going to buy. Yet he has to form his policies in advance. He cannot usually serve customers any other way.
>
> (G. Copeman, *The Chief Executive and Business Growth*, Leviathan House, London, 1971)

important characteristic of managing directors in chapter 4.

Another important aspect of decision-making skills is that, in addition to making the detailed analysis, it is important to keep the wider perspective in view. This was expressed in the following way by one of our MDs:

> There are two critical things that a chief executive has got to have. One is the ability to see both the wood and the trees. If they have not got that, then they should not be there (if they have not got that, they probably will not be there), and then, in other words, having seen the direction, applying and following through on that direction and making it happen.... Seeing the wood and the trees is being able to see what the issues are and not get submerged beneath a mass of paper and issues.

This was more directly expressed by another as follows:

> The main attribute is, I believe, to be able to take an overall view – to see every facet. I may not be able to look at the detail, but I have enough knowledge to be able to see when a thing is important, and I think that that is the main thing.

Sometimes this skill was seen as an ability to recognize trends more quickly than others, as described by this chief executive:

> It is recognizing what is likely to happen rather more quickly than other people; seeing into the future and moving things in that direction before it is obvious that you ought to move in that direction . . . .
>
> It's seeing where whole businesses are moving, what the tendency in the whole of the market is, and what the spin-off is, therefore, for your own company or business, then having the feel to move in that direction. Sometimes it is only a feel, and you can only just start to shift the thing in that direction; then the signs become more obvious, and if you've got it right you find you've started to be pointed in that direction, hopefully, before other people have got there.

Another manifestation was in the form of deeper insight:

> It's being able to see further through a brick wall than the next man, then being able to procure results of whatever sort, by whatever means are most appropriate. Finally – I don't know whether this is a skill – being quite sure that you're certain what you want to do, or don't do it.

Much of this was summed up by one MD as simply being *perceptive*:

> It is important that you are perceptive. You need to be able to get to the core of the problem quickly. You must be able to recognize a developing situation. There are some peripheral things you have to understand, such as numbers; you have to understand what goes towards making a profit. You have to be capable of managing people. You have to understand people.

Managerial Skills

Managing people is a key skill, but not the most important in my view. You must have all those skills. But even if you do, if you are not perceptive enough to recognize the needs of the business – the things that you need to do – and be able to move quickly if you spot things going wrong, then you will not succeed, even if you are the best manager of people in the world.

To another MD, the important thing was to take time for decisions.

> I think I have a lot of common sense. I am persistent. I have a lot of energy . . . . I am not impulsive, either with people or decisions. I don't feel the urge to do something just because someone has brought me a problem. If we have a golden opportunity, I don't find myself rushing into it. It's an ability to stand back and take my time.

All the above reflections have stressed various aspects of decision-making skills – 'analysis', 'overview' and 'follow-through'. One MD, however, did consider the analytical skills to be subsidiary and, while stressing the need to be able to push decisions through, raised another important skill:

> The people who don't make it to do this job [MD] don't necessarily lack analytical skills. This organization is stuffed full of people of intellect and superb analysis. I don't rate myself any more than average in that sense. People fail, in my view, in one of two ways. One is that they are frightened by decisions. The people who stick in the organization [don't get promoted] are those who don't have the guts to push a decision through. It's desperately easy to take a decision. What's more difficult is taking the responsibility to push it through. The other, which is very important, particularly in a large organization, is your ability to stand on your feet and talk – to talk in two ways. One, to make a presentation to your shareholders – the ability to present and sell a case. The other one is to be able to sit around a table and talk articulately and confidently to both shop stewards and one's peers. Some people can talk OK to peers and technologists, but talk down to shop stewards.

> I suggest below three characteristics which I would look, for in a successful top executive. These are, of course, all in addition to an adequate level of competence in his/her career record.
>
> The most important faculty of a senior executive in almost any sphere of activity is that of motivation–self-motivation as well as the ability to persuade people to believe that their grasp is even further than their reach. For it is through that achievement that any society will grow.
>
> The second characteristic for which I look is that of curiosity–the enquiring mind which searches for knowledge which may, not even necessarily will, be used to advantage.
>
> The third attribute, in some ways the most valuable of all, is a lateral-thinking ability and the use of analogy. In the younger senior executive this often proves an early and effective substitute for that breadth of experience which can only be achieved through time.
>
> (Sir Owen Green, Chairman, BTR plc)

Skills with People

Most respondents mentioned interpersonal skills in one form or another, and, while often they mentioned decision-making first, the impression given was that *people skills* were either equally important or a very close second. Often the skill specifically mentioned was, as in the above comment, to do with communication; for example: 'communication skills are also vitally important. I spend 60 per cent of my time in communicating on a wide variety of matters.' Other managing directors expressed the need for good relationships in order to get good performance:

> Working with people is a key skill – knowing how to get the best out of people, by encouragement and example. It needs more confidence to operate in a kindly supportive way than to be controlling. It also needs honesty and patience.

There is possibly even an element of manipulation in this, as one suggested:

Relationships with people are the most important part of it, in the end. This means getting them to do things they would not have thought of doing – possibly, even, things they don't want to do.

There was also an element of the 'autocrat' in many of the responses. For example:

> I appear to have an ability to bring people along with me, but that's only good if you have decided where you want to go. I think I am a fairly genial, gambling, big guy, who wanders around the place, but others see me as autocratic and as someone who makes his own mind up . . . . I will take advice and I will change my mind . . . . I will consult, *as I see necessary*.

This is a theme which will be taken up in more detail in a section on 'consultative style' in chapter 7.

Leadership

Although, as indicated at the beginning of this section, leadership was not mentioned by many respondents, some did see it as an important skill. Sometimes this was expressed in fairly traditional terms, as follows:

> I think you have to lead from the front. I don't think there is any real alternative to that. They have to see me out there pushing their cause. I must be seen to be fighting for the kind of things that we believe to be right . . . .
> They also expect me to give them the kind of direction that they feel comfortable with – in the sense that I don't impose impossible targets; although, if I think there is room for improvement, I will say so. Normally, I sit down with them and discuss problems.

At other times, it was seen more in terms of an ability to influence and organize people, as another MD suggested:

> I don't think there is any doubt that part of the success I have had [in this company] is because I saw an opportunity to influence and was prepared to put in the hours that other people

did not put in. I would go further and say that to some extent my career became a hobby . . . .

From an early age, when I got involved in something, although not necessarily a forceful character, I seemed to end up as captain, or chairman, or team leader. I think this is because I have an organized mind. I can't deal with disorganization. Even my children would say, 'Here comes father – he wants to organize us.' I don't really; it's just that I believe success can be so much greater if targeted and properly organized.

Ability to Learn from Failure

The ability to bounce back from mistakes and failures was mentioned by several people.

> It's surprising how easily many people accept defeat. I think not being prepared to be beaten (a sort of stickability) can carry you through a heck of a long way . . . . It's the non-acceptance of being beaten.

More important, not only is it necessary to be able to bounce back, but one must also learn from one's failures:

> All my own experience tells me that most people will not face up to things that have gone wrong, or they certainly won't face up to analysing what happened and why it happened, and seeing if next time you can avoid it.

This can also be seen as another example of 'determination', which we have mentioned above.

Moderate Risk-Taking

Perhaps the ability to make mistakes and recover from them is related to the degree of risk one is prepared to take. There is also an element of risk in being prepared to make decisions and push them through, although this also relates to the degree of confidence one has in oneself. All our samples came over as highly self-confident. They also in the main saw themselves as moderate risk-takers, as one successful MD relates:

Managerial Skills

> The major characteristics that I look to find in a top executive are:
>
> 1 a thorough professional knowledge of his subject;
> 2 that he should be articulate;
> 3 that he should be literate;
> 4 that he should be decisive, capable of weighing up the pros and cons of the situations that he is going to face and coming to rapid decisions
>
> With any top post it is also important in this day and age that he has a presence, can put his line across, be persuasive, and at the same time demonstrate a firm grip and determination to succeed
>
> (Sir Raymond Lygo, Chief Executive, British Aerospace)

I am a risk-taker — but a very calculated one. I am not a gambler. Also, I have no money in any other person's business. I don't have a lot of confidence in other people's capabilities in other companies. All the money I have got is in my own.

This man had, in fact, recently been involved in a management buy-out and had quite a considerable investment in his company. He did not see this as a risk because of his faith in himself, although as can be seen he does not have a great deal of faith in managers in other companies.

High Work Rate

A few managing directors mentioned an ability to work quickly and efficiently as an important attribute; for example: '[I have an] Enormous work rate, and superimposed on this is an innate academic intelligence to read and interpret written information.' Most made some mention during the interviews of the very high level of paperwork to be got through. Many, in fact, spent several hours a day in reading, often in the evenings. So an ability to handle paperwork quickly would be a considerable advantage.

> In my experience the most important characteristics of a successful managing director are 'helicopter vision' and self-propulsion. Powers of communication, the ability to listen and the ability to lead are additional requirements. But uniquely the managing director must bring the quality of vision for the future of the corporation, which will need to be adjusted as a result of discussions with others. By definition, however, the managing director cannot, in this area, be just a follower of the pack, or a judger of the consensus; he has actually to be capable of making a major personal contribution.
>
> Among personal characteristics, one of the most important is the ability to live with a heavy load of responsibility. One is looking here for people who can still sleep at nights, irrespective of the size of the problems, but who care enough that they will put work considerations before all others, when it is essential.
>
> (Sir John Harvey-Jones, former Chairman, ICI)

Key Areas of Skill

It can be seen from our interviews that there are essentially three main areas of skill which managing directors see as important. One is concerned with *interpersonal skills* – the ability to develop and direct a team of people. Another involves *analytical abilities and decision-making*. The third is about *long-term planning and coping with change*. This involves a visionary quality and is, perhaps, the area which most involves leadership. This trichotomy was very succinctly expressed by one managing director:

There are three main areas:

1 Develop a team of people: get the right chemistry – people working well. Always take an interest in people.
2 You need the ability to analyse proposals and business plans: the ability to pinpoint key factors.

Managerial Skills

3   To be a visionary: this is needed to cope with a changing world and to exploit the future.

These same characteristics are found in a number of other studies. Copeman found in his study of chief executives that by far the greatest number of qualities mentioned as important were concerned with the 'ability to handle people' – selection, motivation and development. The next in frequency were those concerned with the 'ability to analyse business problems', 'develop product policy' and 'create new ideas'. Garfield lists six attributes shared by peak performers:

Missions that motivate: the call to action, the 'click' that starts things moving.
Results in real time: purposeful activity directed at achieving goals that contribute to a mission.
Self-management through self-mastery: the capacity of self-observation and effective thinking.
Team-building/team-playing: the complement to self-management – empowering others to produce.
Course correction: mental agility, concentration, finding and navigating a 'critical path'.
Change management: anticipating and adapting to major change while maintaining momentum and balance within an overall game plan.

W. Bennis lists five 'competencies' which, in a study of US chief executive officers, he found they all possessed:

1   *Vision*: The capacity to create and communicate a compelling vision of a desired state of affairs – to impart clarity to this vision and induce commitment to it.
2   *Communication and alignment*: The capacity to communicate their vision in order to gain the support of their multiple constituencies.
3   *Persistence, consistency, focus*: The capacity to maintain the organization's direction, especially when the going gets rough.

4 *Empowerment*: The capacity to create environments that can tap and harness the energies and abilities necessary to bring about the desired results.
5 *Organizational learning*: The capacity to find ways for the organization to monitor its own performance, compare results with established objectives, have access to a continuously evolving data base on which to review past actions and base future ones, and decide how, if necessary, the organizational structure and key personnel must be abandoned or rearranged when faced with new conditions.

Bennis summarizes this as 'leadership that knows what it wants, communicates those intentions successfully, empowers others, and knows when and how to stay on course and when to change'. All of these listings correspond very closely with the findings of our study, involving, as they do, *vision, communication, leadership* and *persistence*. Item 5 in Bennis's list, *organizational learning*, is also a rather lengthy way of saying: review and learn from your mistakes.

The ability to handle mistakes was also found by McCall and Lombardo to be an important characteristic of successful managers. In comparing managers who had 'arrived' with those who had 'derailed', they point out that neither group made many mistakes, but 'arrivers overwhelmingly handled them with poise and grace. Almost uniformly they admitted the mistake, forewarned others so they wouldn't be blindsided by it, then set about analyzing and fixing it.' They also noted that 'arrivers' were particularly good at focusing on problems and solving them, and had high interpersonal skills. Hall and Donnell also noted in their article on 'Managerial achievement' that high-achieving managers rated themselves, and were perceived by their subordinates, as very significantly more interpersonally competent than low or average achievers.

Many other studies have endorsed the importance of critical thinking for success in management. In *The Professional Decision-Thinker*, B Heirs stresses that good decisions can only be made if thinking is well organized prior to the decision,

Managerial Skills

and also that good decision-making is a team effort. The good manager is, therefore, the leader of a 'thinking team'. Many of the MDs in our study did, in fact, see themselves in this sort of role. An open-minded approach is also a key factor in good thinking. In a paper on 'Dogmatism and managerial achievement', J. M. Close found first-line and lower-middle managers to be significantly more dogmatic than upper-middle and top managers. He suggests that the open-minded personality has a greater chance of reaching higher levels in the organization than does its relatively close-minded counterpart. This will be part of the successful manager's 'value system' (see chapter 5). To be an effective decision-maker, it is necessary to be open to new information, ideas and changes in the world.

Much of what we have said about decision-making is summed up by what H. Muller has called *helicopter quality* (a term he had, in fact, borrowed from van Lennep). In *The Search for the Qualities Essential to Advancement in a Large Industrial Group*, he defined it as:

(a) A man's ability to look at his problems from a higher vantage point and shape his work accordingly on the basis of a personal vision.
(b) The urge and ability to place facts and problems within a broader context, by immediately detecting relevant relationships with systems of wider scope.

Muller found this to be the key quality that correlated with managerial success, in terms of promotion through the organization. It was also clearly the key quality that our managing directors saw in themselves.

Managers or Leaders

It has recently become fashionable to distinguish between 'management' and 'leadership'. In fact, as far back as 1977 A. Zalenznik suggested that there is a clear distinction in orientation between leaders and managers in their conception of work, their attitude towards others and their orientation to goals. More recently, in *Leaders*, Bennis and Nanus made a similar distinction:

> Management typically consists of a set of contractual exchanges, 'you do this job for that reward' . . . . What gets exchanged is not trivial: jobs, security, money. The result at best is compliance; at worst, you get a spiteful obedience. The end result of the leadership we have advanced is completely different: it is empowerment. Not just higher profits and wages, which usually accompany empowerment, but an organisational culture that helps employees generate a sense of meaning in their work and a desire to challenge themselves to experience success. Leadership stands in the same relation to empowerment that management does to compliance.

This makes leadership seem like something good and desirable, while mere managmeent is distinctly inferior, if not downright anti-social, but it does not really tell us what leadership is. Many social scientists have attempted definitions. In *Psychology and Effective Behaviour* J. C. Coleman, for example, says it consists of:

1. *Structuring the situation* – making it clear where the group is going and what has to be done.
2. *Controlling group behaviour* – creating and enforcing appropriate rules for guiding the behaviour of group members.
3. *Speaking for the group* – sensing and articulating (both internally and externally) the objectives and feelings of the group.
4. *Helping the group to achieve its goals and potential* – mobilizing and co-ordinating group resources and decision making.

We think that many 'managers' would subscribe to all four of the above activities as an integral part of their job. There are

Managerial Skills

Manager	Leader
Relations with others	
Relates to others according to their role	Relates in a more intuitive and emphatic way
Prefers high probability of winning and low probability of losing	Willing to risk losing if rewards for winning are high
Communicates to subordinates indirectly through the system	Communicates directly
Perceived by others as detached and manipulative	Attracts strong feelings of identity
Conserves what is traditional and current	Exerts influence for change
Goals	
Goals arise out of necessities	Goals arise out of desires
Goals are deeply embedded in history and culture of the organization	Goals focus on the need for change
Strategy assumes more importance than the goal	Strategy is the means to a goal
Focuses on strategy, structure and systems	Focuses on style, staff, skills and shared goals
Conceptions of work	
Values tradition	Seeks change and new ideas
Instinct for survival dominates need for risk	Accepts risk where opportunities and rewards are high
Delegates cautiously	Delegates freely–has faith in people
Analytical and methodical	Intuitive
Maintains control over people and ideas	Encourages autonomy
Reactive	Proactive
Identifies totally with the organization	Works in the organization but can stand outside it

(This is a slightly edited version of a table given by M. Sorcher, *Predicting Executive Success*, Wiley, New York, 1985, based on the writings of A. Zaleznik, 'Managers and leaders: are they different?, *Harvard Business Review*, May–June 1977, and C. Watson, 'Leadership, management and the seven keys', *The McKinsey Quarterly*, Autumn 1983) also strong echos of Mintzberg's managerial roles, which were outlined at the start of this chapter. Goldsmith and Clutterbuck, writing in a more specifically managerial context, give three important elements of leadership:

1 Leaders are visible.
2 Leaders provide a clear mission, which they believe in passionately themselves and incite others to subscribe to .
3 Leadership thrives where people have clear objectives and the resources to strike out after them.

The principal addition provided by this definition is the notion that leaders (at any rate in the management context) have a sense of mission.

Although the managing directors in our survey did not talk much about leadership, reading into their perceptions of their key skills, it is obvious that they see themselves as having all the skills necessary to fulfil that role. In fact, it is obvious that, for them, leadership is an integral part of management. Perhaps the distinction is only in the minds of academics.

> Courage; the ability to make decisions; to take calculated risks; to say no, and to remove people who are not effective. Self-discipline, and both physical and mental toughness, with the ability to switch off; a determination to be up front in dealing with competition; empathy–the ability to see things from other persons' point of view without necessarily agreeing; the ability to be articulate and to be a good listener as well as to communicate clearly; consistency; the ability to stand up to pressures; to be objective; to be calm in a storm; a personality that pleases; a conceptual ability, which includes the capacity to think things through; and, above all, common sense.
> (P. F. Scott, President, Provincial Insurance plc)

Managerial Skills

Summary

Successful managing directors require skills in three main areas. These all overlap and interact with each other. The area they nearly always mention first and seem to see as a key skill is that of *problem-solving* and *decision-making*. This involves analytical skills and the ability to see relationships and spot trends. It also involves the ability to 'follow through' and get the decision implemented; this is particularly important where the decision is unpopular or has unpleasant consequences – such as redundancies. The second area of importance is *skills with people* – the ability to select and manage a team and, particularly, to keep them working well together, even when the going gets tough. Thirdly, they need a vision of the future – where is the organization going, how will it look in ten or twenty years time? – and the ability to communicate to and enthuse others with this vision. These skills are essentially those of leadership.

7
MANAGEMENT PHILOSOPHY

A few years ago, one of the authors was an examiner for a professional institute connected with management which included a paper on organizational behaviour in its qualifying examinations. He was fascinated, and appalled, by the underlying assumptions which showed through many of the candidates' papers. Admittedly they were mostly quite young, but they appeared to be working on an assumption that 'management' was mainly a matter of shouting orders to a waiting band of willing but not very bright workers, who would then scurry off to do their master's bidding. The manager's *right to manage* was one of their favourite expressions. We use this story to illustrate what we mean by 'management philosophy'. It is concerned with the underlying beliefs and assumptions which a manager holds about people and about how to manage in organizations. A manager's philosophy will be very much influenced by his values, particularly those concerning people and relationships (discussed in chapter 5). The philosophy outlined above seems to be based on an assumption that one part of the community (i.e. the managers) have some sort of right to order about another part (i.e. the workers), who then do as they are told. This is, of course, an extremely naïve view in the late 1980s, but was probably held by many in the nineteenth century. What is depressing is that it was still held recently by a number of people embarking on a career in a profession from which many managers are drawn.

Management Philosophy

A more sophisticated analysis of two management philosophies was given by Douglas McGregor in *The Human Side of Enterprise*, which, although published in 1960, is still very relevant today. Essentially, *theory X* (see box on page 108) takes a mechanistic view of organizations and does not value subordinates as people, seeing them simply as units in the production process. This philosophy will lead to an authoritarian management style. *Theory Y* values all members of the organization as potential contributors and will lead to a more participative style.

Another way of looking at management philosophy, which has a long pedigree, is about whether the manager is more concerned with *people* or with the *task* in hand, or a combination of both. This approach originated with work at the Ohio State University and the University of Michigan, but is best known by managers in the form presented by Blake and Mouton in *The Managerial Grid*. Their grid can be used to classify managers according to the degree of emphasis they place on either of the two dimensions – 'concern for people' and 'concern for production'. According to Blake and Mouton, the most effective managers will score high on both.

An individual's management philosophy is, then, concerned with how his value system influences the way he manages in organizations. It is expressed in terms of his attitudes to people, particularly his subordinates, and how he sets about organizing production. It will influence how he uses the skills, discussed in the preceding chapter.

Diagnosing Management Philosophy

Since management philosophy can have such a powerful impact on how the individual manages, it is obviously interesting and important to try to discover if there is any consistency in the philosophies of successful managing directors. We attempted to do this by asking the direct question, 'What is your management philosophy?' This seemed to be perfectly intelligible and produced clear answers, although sometimes

> *McGregor's theory X and theory Y*
>
> In *The Human Side of Enterprise,* Douglas McGregor suggests that the way in which a manager manages will depend very largely upon the assumptions that he makes about the work in general and his subordinates in particular. He defined two possible sets of assumptions that managers might use. He labelled these theory X and theory Y. He chose these as neutral labels so as not to imply any value judgement between them, though in many ways McGregor's own value preference for theory Y shines clearly through his writing. The two sets of assumptions are summarized briefly below:
>
> 1 *Theory X assumptions.* Most people, it is assumed, dislike work and will avoid it if they can. Work is therefore a 'necessary evil'. Most people dislike responsibility, require direction and control, have little ambition and require security above all else.
> 2 *Theory Y assumptions.* These are more complex and include the beliefs that most people are naturally active and enjoy achieving goals (particularly those they have set themselves); that commitment to objectives is related to the rewards associated with their achievement; that ingenuity, imagination and creativity are widely distributed in the population; and that people will accept and seek responsibility
>
> It is important to remember that these are not statements of what 'people' are really like but statements of what managers may believe 'people' or their subordinates are like. The beliefs are not usually too consciously articulated by the manager, but can be inferred from his behaviour in the way in which he manages. A manager holding theory X assumptions will have a choice of either one of two styles, or he can use a mixture of both. Since in his view people do not want to work, he can get them to produce by coercion, using threats and punishments (hard-line X), or he can seduce people into work by offering 'bribes' or rewards, such as piece rates, bonuses and competitions (soft-line X). Both these approaches are based on the same underlying assumptions and have much in common. Both require precise definition of the work to be done, and close control and checks to ensure the required standards have been met.

Management Philosophy

> Theory Y assumptions will give rise to a much more open and flexible style of managing. Since people are seen as active and co-operative, the manager's role is to ensure that work is co-ordinated, and that organizational goals are clear and compatible with those of the individual. It will, in general, be a much more participative style

additional probing was needed to produce greater clarity. Some MDs also completed the Leadership Orientation Questionnaire. The results from this will be discussed later in this chapter. We were particularly interested to see if responses would tend towards person or task orientations, or a combination of both. One problem is that so much has been written, and taught on courses, about these dimensions that there is a danger that only the 'correct' or socially desirable answers will be given. We could guard against this only by listening carefully for the underlying meaning behind the words, and then probing further if there seemed to be slight inconsistencies. It is also the case that there is really no reason for men in the position of these MDs to be concerned about giving socially correct answers. As might be expected, they all came over to us as very self-confident and willing to express opinions regardless of social convention.

Concern for people	High concern for people Low concern for production (soft-line theory X) (Country-club management, 1.9)	High concern for people High concern for production (theory Y) (team management, 9.9)
	Low concern for people Low concern for production (apathetic management, 1.1)	Low concern for people High concern for production (hard-line theory X) (scientific management, 9.1)

Concern for production

The managerial grid

Blake and Mouton have taken two dimensions of management concern derived from earlier studies—namely, concern for people and concern for production. They have arranged them orthogonally as the two dimensions of a grid, as in the previous diagram. Each axis is marked as a nine-point scale. Thus it is theoretically possible to identify any manager's style of relating to his subordinates with two co-ordinates indicating his position on the grid. They then identified and discussed certain extreme styles, as follows:

1.9 management. This manager has a very high concern for people, but has a low concern for production. His assumption is that attention to the needs of people, the avoidance of conflict and developing good human relations will automatically encourage good work. Blake calls this *country-club* management, since the objective is to keep everyone happy, as in a country club. It is similar to soft-line theory X in approach. The danger, he suggests, is that everyone is so busy being comfortable and happy that little production may take place

9.1 management. This manager has a high concern for production but a low concern for people. Blake calls him a *scientific* manager because he sees his role in terms of scheduling work and machines and will tend to be strongly influenced by 'scientific' techniques of production scheduling, such as critical-path analysis and operations research. He sees people as simply units in the production process. This style is similar to hard-line theory X. The danger is that the high emphasis on production and control will produce high conflict and creativity to beat the system on the part of subordinates, so that output will not, in fact, be optimized.

1.1 management. This is the *apathetic* manager who shows low concern both for people and for production. His approach is simply to put in the minimum effort to meet organizational requirements. It is a style unlikely to produce high output. Some writers have typified this type of manager as WIB (weak, inefficient, bastard).

5.5 management. This is the *compromiser* who believes that the way in which to achieve success is to balance the needs of people against the need to produce. Blake's view is that while aiming for the best of two worlds he may, as is always the risk with compromise, end up with the worst. He may not put sufficient emphasis on people to achieve the loyalty inspired by the 1.9 manager, or sufficient emphasis on production to achieve the pay-offs of the scientific approach of the 9.1 manager.

9.9 management. Blake calls this *team* management, where the approach is on achieving 'production through people'. The emphasis is on developing an interdependent team with high trust and commitment to organizational goals. This is very similar to McGregor's notion of theory Y management. The basic assumption, made by Blake, is that 9.9 is the best and most effective style.

A more difficult problem to deal with is that there may be a difference between the *espoused theory* – what a person says (and believes) he is doing – and the *theory in use* – what a person is actually doing. There is a lot of evidence that managers frequently espouse one theory, but that what they do is more consistent with another. If asked, most managers say they espouse theory Y, but very often their behaviour is more consistent with theory X. It is only possible to infer the 'theory in use' from observation of what managers actually do. In an interview study such as this, what we were recording was, obviously, the 'espoused theory'. One can only make inferences about the 'theory in use' from inconsistencies in what is said or from descriptions of actual incidents. We have tried to do this where possible.

Person Orientation

Within the traditional framework of person versus task orientation, most of our MDs appeared to favour a primarily person-oriented approach when describing their philosophy, although they were also obviously concerned with the performance of the organization, as this MD illustrates:

> In general, my management philosophy is to start from the assumption that a business, a company, an organization, has a character, a personality of its own. That character and that personality are made up from the people who work for the company – not just the top people, but everybody who works for it. I am therefore very conscious of this as a factor in the success or failure of the company. So I think very much in terms of how people fit in, how people fit with each other – the team effect – and it is very important that we are a sympathetic organization to work for. We have been able to avoid becoming just a hard-nosed, tough, modern organization. This does not detract from our efficiency.

In general, they saw themselves as achieving task performance through their role as a team leader – virtually the classic 9.9 style of Blake and Mouton, as this chief executive highlights:

> I am person oriented – 65 per cent of my effort is on people, 35 per cent on technical and future planning . . . .
> I would summarize my management philosophy as 'to encourage people to use whatever talents they may have in the best possible way'.

We are not sure how much this is a real reflection of their style, or simply an expression of an 'ideal', as the balance between the two approaches was often only brought out after probing by the interviewers. But we have some indications of an underlying tendency towards an authoritarian approach (this has also been noted in other sections), as this MD's comments reflect:

> Put your trust in people. Select the right people – trust them and give them responsibility. People will then work for you, because they can't let you down. But you must be good at assessing people, and not be soft. If people are not good enough, you must say so.

Management Philosophy

Another MD expressed his approach as very clearly a matter of delegating authority and responsibility:

> I believe in giving managers authority and responsibility to do the job, with tolerance of people who make decisions and make mistakes. I don't like people who won't make decisions. I think I am very demanding to those people who don't learn from their mistakes, and probably a little intolerant, but I think also, if you were to ask other people about me, I have an open-door management philosophy. But I am demanding.

Task Orientation

A significant minority of chief executives did express management philosophies which seem to be more oriented towards task concerns:

> Be clear on objectives and then go for them. Objectives are most important, and it is necessary to understand constraints.

One MD saw it very clearly in terms of getting the task right first, and the people aspects would follow:

> Essentially you've got to get the right product, the right quality, the right costs, the right delivery, the right after-sales service and the right marketing. These are the six things that I talk about . . . .
> They are not 'people things' in themselves, but you need people to develop and achieve these things . . . .
> There is an old navy expression, 'An efficient ship is a happy ship', *not* 'A happy ship is an efficient ship'. I absolutely believe that. I think if a company is efficient, and is seen to be efficient, and is seen to be doing well, then people who work for it respond and become very proud of it, which in turn increases their effectiveness – but the efficiency comes first, so to speak.

In another case, the MD saw his role as being 'to cope with the future':

> It's about long-term thinking – where the organization is going . . . . The principal thing that management is about is

successfully coping with change. I really do think that is fundamental to my management philosophy . . . . That's what we really are all here for at the end of the day – the bottom line, it's all about managing change.

There was also the occasional case of a somewhat paternalistic approach, as illustrated by this MD:

> Obviously I am employed by the shareholders to obtain the best possible results that I can for them, but consistently. I have to try to retain a type of paternalism within the company, because it has still got a lot of the elements of the family company, and staff genuinely respond to it. I find it almost an embarrassment . . . .
> It is also about determining priorities between customers, shareholders and staff.

Another expression of this was as follows:

> When you look at decisions, you've got to make a decision using your brain, but in implementing that decision always use your heart as well. That is not to say you divorce it like that – you can't. The two are integrally related, but you must have compassion and consideration for people in implementing your decisions.

Task and Person Orientation

As noted above, there were very few spontaneous expressions of a philosophy which really placed an equal emphasis on both task and process; even those that recognized some balance between these factors were far from participative in approach:

> To open up the decision-making process as much as possible, trying to get, not necessarily a consensus decision, but a decision which everyone is comfortable with and believes is right. This can be a lengthy process – similar to the Japanese system – but it gets commitment. It also means that if you do have to take a decision on your own it will be accepted, because your colleagues and subordinates know you only did this because the situation made it necessary.

Another illustration was provided by this chief executive:

Management Philosophy

I think to be successful in management you've got to be prepared to be courageous. You've got to be prepared to see the way ahead and at the end of the day be prepared to take the decision as to where you are going to go. One factor in many senior managers is that they are afraid of taking risk decisions . . . .

I think the other management philosophy is that, in coming to that decision, you have got to be wise enough to gather around you a good team of people, who you respect and who have the right mix of abilities . . . .

At the end of the day the risk decision will always be yours, but you need a good cabinet around you to help you crystallize out on what that decision is going to be.

An example of a fairly 'hard-nosed' attitude was given by the managing director of a group of companies, who saw his role as a mentor to his senior managers, but with a fairly tough approach:

To be godfather to senior managers. You've got to be policeman, helpmate, nurse, adviser, shoulder to cry on, guide, mentor, etc . . . .

I must not get too deeply into areas of weakness, because I am only interested in results, and the minute I start to understand their problems it means I start to tolerate them. When I start to tolerate them it means I become less effective as a manager.

Open Management

Equally with the emphasis on managing people was a belief in an 'open style' of management, although this had slightly different meanings to different people. In some cases it simply meant disseminating information from the centre, so that people know what is going on:

I try to run this business as openly as possible. We try to publish as much as we possibly can. We only retain things that are commercially sensitive; other than that, we tell people – employees – as much as we can about the business, the bad news and the good news, because I think, if people recognize you as an honest individual who is willing to sit down and talk to them about the business as a whole, they will react positively.

A popular phrase was 'open-door management style'. This usually meant that employees could come and talk about problems or grievances, and it was seen as a way of keeping open channels of communication with what is going on in the organization, as this MD reflected:

> I talk to everyone in the company. My door is always open. I encourage them to come and talk to me. Sometimes I wish I hadn't – it can waste a lot of time – but I find I can discover problems quickly. If people are happy to come and talk to me about problems without my being nasty or aggressive, then I get more out of those people.

Consultative Style

Despite the emphasis on openness and the need to involve people, there was, as noted above, very little evidence as a truly participative style. Virtually universally, these MDs saw themselves as responsible for the final decision, after perhaps quite a lot of consultation:

> My management style is open and informal, but not particularly democratic. I listen to what everybody has to say, but on all the boards that I have been MD we have never voted. I listen and then I make the decision.

Sometimes the style was even more towards a 'selling' approach, where the purpose of the discussion is to convince subordinates of the correctness of top management decisions and to develop their commitment to them.

> I believe in an open-management style and involving people. We must in the future achieve levels of performance that we have not yet achieved. I am convinced that there is no way we are going to do this unless people are led to understand what we are really trying to do. They must feel that they are

involved, that they have been participants in making the decision. This necessitates an open style. In our own company we are well down that track. We divulge information to an extent we just would not have dreamed of, even ten years ago.

In answer to a question from the interviewer, 'Does this mean simply telling people what is happening or involving them in the decision?', he replied:

> In their own way I think people should be encouraged to understand and encouraged to give their opinions. In the final analysis, management has to manage, but I don't think that management can, any more, sit in the boardroom in its ivory tower, and made decisions and hand them down. Management has to carry the workforce with them in decisions which they have to make. It is not a shared responsibility.

On all but a minority of occasions, the tendency was even more towards a distinctively, although delicate, authoritarian style, as illustrated by this MD:

> It is important that people should know what is expected of them . . . . It is very important to give people clear responsibility and accountability and then let them get on with it . . . .
> It's like pulling on a piece of elastic. You've got to keep people with you, but you must not pull it so hard that it breaks.

Only in very few cases did there seem to be any real reciprocity in the way in which top managers interacted with subordinates, and even here there seemed to be a certain caution and reluctance to trust, totally, the good sense of others:

> Before you can manage you have got to learn to be the servant of those you manage – all the time. If you actually do that, you then get more feedback than anybody else. It's not a calculated thing – you have to mean it and believe it. So you are never left in the dark. You are never isolated by anybody. In fact, a lot of the so-called intuitions that you get are actually warnings that you get from other people . . . .

You've got to expose yourself and be totally open and ready to receive everything that is coming back in. That is being a servant, in my view . . . . It is being totally open to other people and willing to help them all the time – as long as you think that what they want is a rational, sensible thing for the good of the business.

I am very people oriented – although you need enough technical and financial knowledge to know when you are being taken for a ride.

The Leadership Opinion Questionnaire

The Leadership Opinion Questionnaire (LOQ), developed by E. A. Fleishman measures two dimensions of leadership or management style – *consideration* and *structure*. These concepts arose from research on the behaviour of supervisors, carried out at Ohio State University. They are defined by Fleishman as follows:

> *Consideration.* Reflects the extent to which an individual is likely to have job relationships with subordinates characterized by mutual trust, respect for ideas, consideration of their feelings, and a certain warmth between the individual and them. A high score [on the questionnaire] is indicative of a climate of good rapport and two-way communication. A low score indicates the individual is likely to be more impersonal in relations with group members.
> *Structure.* Reflects the extent to which an individual is likely to define and structure his or her own role and those of subordinates toward *goal attainment*. A high score on this dimension characterizes individuals who play a very active role in directing group activities through planning, communicating information, scheduling, criticizing, trying out new ideas, and so forth. A low score characterizes individuals who are likely to be relatively inactive in giving direction in these ways.

These dimensions are independent of each other, so that any particular manager can score high on one and low on the other, or high or low on both.

Management Philosophy

We asked the managing directors who took part in our study if they would complete the LOQ. Twenty-nine of them agreed to do so. Most of them scored high on both dimensions. For *consideration*, the mean score was 56.3, with a range of 40–78. The mean score for executives in general is 55; 62 per cent of the chief executives scored more than this. For *structure*, the mean score was 54, with a range of 41–67. This compares with a mean score for the general population of executives of 51; 75 per cent of our sample of MDs scored more than this. In other words, most chief executives are more concerned than other managers with making clear to subordinates both exactly what is expected of them and what they themselves can be expected to do. They are also more likely to show warmth, trust and respect for their subordinates. This is totally consistent with the strong *person orientation* emerging from the interviews, which was coupled with *concern for task*. In fact, the questionnaire produced a very similar picture to the interviews, since a high score on 'consideration' would indicate high person orientation and a high 'structure' score would equate with high concern for task. While, as already indicated, scores were relatively high on both dimensions, only six MDs scored higher on 'structure' than on 'consideration', and four had equal scores. Nineteen (65 per cent) scored higher on 'consideration'.

A Philosophy of Openness and Rationality

In attempting to determine the underlying philosophy of the managing directors in our study, it is, in fact, very hard to distinguish the 'espoused theory' from the 'theory in use'. Most saw themselves as very person oriented and described their role as that of a team leader, getting things done through their management team. At first sight this is very persuasive and fits with much of modern management theory and research. Hall and Donnell, for example, found in their article on 'Managerial achievement' that high-achieving managers were more oriented towards theory Y than to theory X assumptions. Low and average achievers did not show this distinction and tended towards theory X. Hall and Donnell described them as oriented towards theory X, but tempered by human-relations training or social desirability. In terms of Blake and Mouton's managerial grid, high achievers showed high task and relationship orientations – the classic 9.9 position. Average achievers showed high task and low relationship orientations (9.1 position). Low achievers scored low on both (1.1). This is perfectly consistent with Blake and Mouton's theory. The problem is that all these are also self-perceptions, although there was some external confirmation, in that high achievers were seen by their subordinates to be considerably more participative than low achievers.

In *The New Competitors*, D. Q. Mills makes the point that many managers place a high emphasis on teamwork, and that if this is the case they must become more participative. Teamwork has the advantage of capitalizing on subordinates' greater involvement with the organization and hence greater contribution in both work and ideas. He quotes the example of People Express as an organization designed primarily from the viewpoint of what people can contribute rather than what the organization requires. However, organizations of this type are still comparative rarities – certainly in Britian – and closer analysis of the attitudes of the MDs we interviewed showed them to be *consultative* rather than *participative*. As G. Copeman found in *The Chief Executive and Business Growth*, they involve people in decisions but retain a lot of the control. Our feeling is that the predominant style is for managers to consult thoroughly, obtaining many views and much information, but then to make the ultimate decision themselves.

> People Express Airlines provides an example of an organization attempting fully to involve all its employees, thus capitalizing on their energy, creativity and commitment.
>
> The most comprehensive and self-conscious effort to fit a business to the capabilities and attitudes of today's work force is being made at People Express Airlines, Inc. This is

Management Philosophy

the first company to try to adapt to today's work force by a radical departure from the traditional concept of a company. The attempt has many intriguing features and has been accompanied by dramatic initial success. In consequence, People Express is the most interesting company in America today.

Don Burr is the company's founder and chief executive officer as well as the mastermind behind the People Express approach. 'We start with certain human values about how we want the company to be run; then we develop a business strategy and link the two up in a powerful way', Burr has commented. Because People Express was a start-up company, Burr was able to think through the link between the business and its people far more fully than if he had been in an ongoing organization. Unfortunately most start-ups fail to take the opportunity that newness offers. Burr seized the opportunity and made it a major element of his business's success.

Most managers begin their thinking with a business purpose and then ask themselves what people the organization will need. At a very early stage, Burr asked this question the other way around. What kind of organization and business can be fitted to the capabilities of the people potentially available to the company?

In many well-managed companies, top managers do ask the question this way for certain key individuals. 'What can we do to get Joan Rollins to come work for us?' they ask. Discussions with Rollins will sometimes fit the organization and its business objectives to her in return for her joining the managerial team. What Burr added to this was his vision of the potential contribution of many individuals much further down in the organization; people who could build a business that would permit them to make the greatest contribution.

Burr combined an opportunity in the airline business with the availability of talented young people and built a company that has sparked a revolution in the airline business. Burr recognized that there are many people in our country yearning for an opportunity to contribute to a company in whose success they can share.

D. Q. Mills, *The New Competitors*, Wiley, New York, 1985)

Apart from the emphasis on people, two other aspects of managerial philosophy came through very strongly. One was concerned with openness. 'An open-door policy' was a much-used phrase, or individuals spoke of being open with information and about future intentions. One reason for this was to develop trust, which is obviously essential for the proper functioning of the organization. As Bennis and Nanus suggest in *Leaders*:

> Trust is the lubrication that makes it possible for organizations to work. It's hard to imagine an *organization* without some semblance of trust operating somehow, somewhere. An organization without trust is more than an anomaly, it's a misnomer, a dim creature of Kafka's imagination. Trust implies accountability, predictability, reliability.

All this is essential to the smooth and efficient running of an organization, and it is also consistent with the high value placed on integrity, discussed in chapter 5. Another aspect of open management is to encourage the flow of information back to the centre, with obvious benefits for decision-making. This is a point made by H. S. Geneen in his autobiography, *Managing*, where he describes the communication system he set up on becoming chief executive of ITT.

The second very strong impression from our interviews is a high emphasis on rationality. This was often coupled with a degree of coolness and distance in interpersonal relationships – sometimes even a little paternalism. Managers felt that people have to be respected and looked after, otherwise they will not work well and will not be committed to the organization; people were not valued for themselves. This is also a little at odds with the espoused value on teamwork. This orientation relates to the high emphasis placed, by our sample, on analytical abilities (discussed in chapter 6). Interestingly, as an example of this, one man compared his style with the Japanese approach of working to a consensus. As Miyajima and Cox have suggested in *A Transactional Analysis of Manager – Subordinate Relationships in both British and Japanese Cultures*, there is an

Management Philosophy

This extract from Geneen's autobiography, describing his approach to communications in ITT, illustrates the importance which many chief executives place on open communication

I announced loudly, clearly, and often that I wanted open communications throughout ITT. Many chief executives say that, but they follow through only to limited degrees. At ITT, it took years to get a new system in place which would cut through the formal structure so that the managers of our autonomous subsidiaries would think of ITT as one company, one team, one group of management men heading in the same direction. We set up a system of monthly reports from our operating divisions, and we augmented our headquarters staff so that we had expert and experienced staff people to check on all facets of our work in telecommunications, electronics, consumer goods, engineering, accounting, legal, marketing, whatever. Our basic and primary policy then became a system in which any staff man could go anywhere in the company and ask any kind of questions and get any kind of answers he could and he could report his findings straight to my office. The only proviso was that he had to inform the manager inolved exactly what he was doing before he sent his report upstairs. He did not need his superior's permission to send the report, but he could not act behind the man's back. He had to give the manager involved a chance to correct the situation. If they could agree on a solution, it got no further. If they could not agree, their dispute would be settled at the headquarters level. I wanted anyone with an idea for improving the company's performance to be able to send it up to my office. I also insisted that every report had to be signed by the man who wrote it. His superior could initial the report and add his comments. But if I had questions, I wanted to talk to the man who wrote the report, not to his superior who might have signed it. I really wanted to know what was going on in the company. I thought it was essential.

(H. S. Geneen with A. Moscow, *Managing*, Grafton Books, London, 1985)

important difference between British and Japanese management philosophies. The British value *professionalism*, which involves rationality and authoritarian control. The Japanese, while still valuing logic and competence, place a much higher value on *warmth and closeness* with colleagues and subordinates than do the British. This is a manifestation of the Japanese 'groupism'. Our managing directors were, clearly, in the British tradition of approaching the world with logic and a stiff upper lip.

> The most important characteristic [for top managers] is leadership–visible leadership based on clear communication of intent. This must be combined with an ability to make decisions in a timely fashion and accept responsibility for those decisions.
>
> Responsiveness to people, including the ability to listen to customers and colleagues alike, is essential and must be matched by a willingness to make his own judgements on what he learns.
>
> A pre-eminent requirement is to create a climate where one's colleagues feel totally free to present their views and fight for their causes, free of corporate politics.
> (Sir David Plastow, Managing Director and Chief Executive, Vickers plc)

Summary

In summary, British managing directors perceive themselves as *person oriented*, in the sense that they see themselves achieving results through their leadership of people. They have a clear view of their objectives and the task requirements. Many emphasize an open-management philosophy, which essentially means being honest and letting people know what you are doing. Alongside this, and despite talking of being open and involving people, these chief executives very clearly see themselves as in charge and personally responsible for major decisions. In *Leaders We Deserve*, Alistair Mant describes this as an 'autocratic management style disguised as participative'. Cooper and Hingley, in *The Change Makers*, also found that 'people in top jobs are decisive, they are also self-revealing, open and communicative'. These descriptions seem to fit the managing directors in our study very well. It is a management philosophy which could be described as *open rationality*.

8
Personality

Personality is a word frequently used in everyday conversation. We may say 'X is lacking in personality', meaning he strikes us as rather insipid, or 'Y has a very dynamic personality', conveying an image of energy and activity. Everyone knows what is meant by it, and there is usually no problem about using the word in this type of context. Strangely, however, it is very difficult to define precisely what is meant by the term 'personality', and hence to define exactly what it is that we are talking about. It obviously has something to do with the impact or impression a person makes; the way he or she relates to others and the environment. This meaning is reflected in the derivation of the word, which is from the Latin *persona*, the mask worn by Roman actors to convey the role they were playing. As used by modern psychologists, the term has a somewhat wider connotation. Perhaps the best way to think of it is the total effect of all the skills, abilities, attributes and experiences of the individual. This means that the characteristics such as motivation, values and skills, which we have discussed in earlier chapters, are all part of personality. We can think of these as special aspects we have picked out to look at separately. In this chapter we are dealing with some of the others.

Apart from the difficulty of definition, there are a number of other problems in dealing with personality (most of which we are going to sidestep in this chapter). The most important of these are:

> *Personality*
>
> Personality, as studied by the psychologist, may be defined as the characteristics and ways of behaving that determine a person's unique adjustments to the environment. The fact that a man eats, sleeps and works does not define his personality; his personality is defined by what he eats, how he sleeps, and what is distinctive about his work patterns. Hence individuality and uniqueness are essential to the definition. What a man does in a given environmental context because of the kind of person he is, beyond the predictions that can be made from context alone, is a reflection of his personality, however it is defined.
>
> Students of personality stress in particular those personal characteristics that affect an individual's ability to get along with other people and with himself. These characteristics are important in the individual's personal adjustment, in his maintenance of self-respect. Any description of the individual personality must take into account appearance, abilities, motives, emotional reactivity, and the residues from earlier experiences that have shaped the person as we find him. The term 'personality' is thus widely inclusive, but it is not synonymous with all of psychology, because it refers specifically to the given individual as he differs from other men.
>
> From *Introduction to Psychology*, 5th edn, by E.R. Hilgard et al., copyright 1971 by Harcourt Brace Jovanovich Inc. New York.
> Reprinted by permission of the publisher.

1 Is personality an attribute of the individual or something to do with the interaction of the individual and the environment—particularly other people? If personality is interactive, it makes no sense to talk about it without specifying the context. This is not too much of a problem here, since the context is clear—managing directors in their organization.

2 Is personality a stable characteristic, or can it vary over time? Commonsense observation confirms that for some people personality does vary. Some people are very different at different times or in different situations. Others are always the same, whenever or wherever you meet them. In fact, this actual variability from 'unpredictable' to 'stable' is an aspect

of personality. In this chapter we are assuming that personality is reasonably stable within the context of work in organizations. Some of the managing directors may also be much the same outside work, others may be very different. We have no data on this.

3 Is personality an inborn characteristic or something which is learned? The significance of this is that, if personality is learned, it will not change. In our view, it is probably a combination of both but many eminent psychologists have lined up on either side of the argument. In the case of this study it probably does not matter, since, even if personality is learned, the main learning occurs very early in life, and for most people very little change occurs after they become adult.

For the purposes of this study, then, we are considering personality to be a reasonably stable characteristic of the person, within a given setting (organizations), which will be one of the major determinants of how a person relates to others. It will obviously be an important contributor to overall success in the role of chief executive.

Measuring Personality

There are two main approaches to measuring and defining particular personalities. First, there are *type theories* which attempt to classify individuals as one out of a range of classes or types. Eysenck, for instance, has suggested a four-part classification based on whether a person is an *extrovert* or an introvert, and whether he or she is *stable* or *emotional(unstable)*. This gives four types: *stable extrovert, unstable extrovert, stable introvert* and *unstable introvert* (see figure 8.1). The second approach is via *trait theory*. In this approach, the psychologist seeks to define an individual's personality by placing him or her on each of a series of dimensions, known as *traits*. In this case, introversion/extroversion or stable/emotional would simply be one of a possible range of traits. Others could be *sociable/unsociable, loyal/fickle* or *wise/foolish*. Many hundreds of

Personality

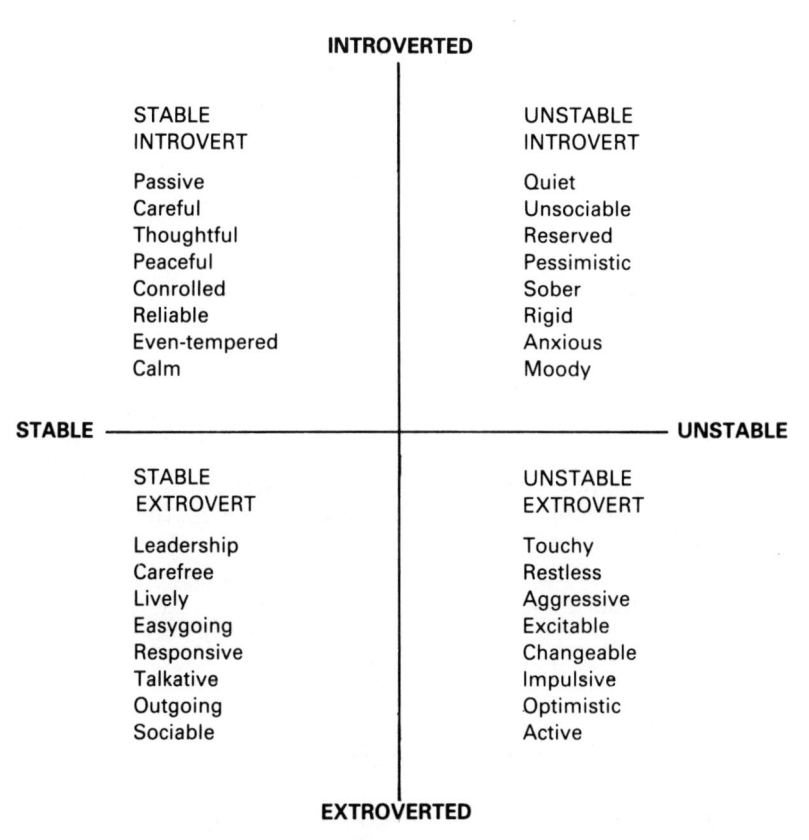

```
                    INTROVERTED
                         |
        STABLE           |    UNSTABLE
        INTROVERT        |    INTROVERT
                         |
        Passive          |    Quiet
        Careful          |    Unsociable
        Thoughtful       |    Reserved
        Peaceful         |    Pessimistic
        Controlled       |    Sober
        Reliable         |    Rigid
        Even-tempered    |    Anxious
        Calm             |    Moody
                         |
STABLE ——————————————————+—————————————————— UNSTABLE
                         |
        STABLE           |    UNSTABLE
        EXTROVERT        |    EXTROVERT
                         |
        Leadership       |    Touchy
        Carefree         |    Restless
        Lively           |    Aggressive
        Easygoing        |    Excitable
        Responsive       |    Changeable
        Talkative        |    Impulsive
        Outgoing         |    Optimistic
        Sociable         |    Active
                         |
                    EXTROVERTED
```

FIGURE 8.1 Eysenck's personality types

trait characteristics can be found in the literature, and it is possible to select and measure those which are appropriate for whatever purpose the study is being made, and produce a profile of the individual. In *The Scientific Analysis of Personality* R.B. Cattell has shown that it is possible to define an individual's personality fairly comprehensively, with a range of sixteen major traits (or factors), each of which is itself a cluster of related traits.

In this study we have used the trait approach, because we believe it gives more flexibility, in that we can select and measure what we see to be relevant managerial traits. There

Cattell's sixteen personality factors (16PF)

	LOW SCORE DESCRIPTION	HIGH-SCORE DESCRIPTION
A	*Reserved*, detached, critical aloof	*Outgoing*, warm hearted, easygoing, participating
A	*Less intelligent*, concrete-thinking	*More Intelligent*, abstract-thinking, bright
C	*Affected by feelings*, emotionally less stable, easily upset	*Emotionally stable*, faces reality, calm, mature
E	*Humble*, mild, accommodating, conforming	*Assertive*, agressive, stubborn, competetive
F	*Sober*, prudent, serious, taciturn	*Happy-go-lucky*, impulsively lively, enthusiastic
G	*Expedient*, disregards rules, feels few obligations	*Concientious*, persevering, staid, moralistic
H	*Shy*, restrained, timid	*Venturesome*, socially bold, uninhibited, spontaneous
I	*Tough-minded*, self-reliant, realistic, no-nonsense	*Tender-minded*, clinging, overprotected, sensitive
L	*Trusting*, adaptable, free of jealousy, easy to get along with	*Suspicious*, self-opinionated, hard to fool
M	*Practical*, careful, conventional, regulated by external realities	*Imaginative*, wrapped up in inner urgencies, careless of practical matters, bohemian

Cattell's sixteen personality factors (continued)

N	*Forthright*, natural, artless, unpretentious	*Shrewd*, calculating, worldly, penetrating
O	*Self-assured*, confident, serene	*Apprehensive*, self-reproaching, worrying, troubled
Q1	*Conservative*, respecting established ideas, tolerant of traditional difficulties	*Experimenting*, liberal, free thinking, radical
Q2	*Group-dependent*, a 'joiner' and sound follower	*Self-sufficient*, prefers own decisions, resourceful
Q3	*Undisciplined self-conflict*, follows own urges, careless of protocol	*Controlled*, socially precise, following self-image
Q4	*Relaxed* tranquil, unfrustrated	*Tense*, frustrated, driven, overwrought

is also a problem with typologies in that people often do not fit neatly into the categories. The trait approach avoids this problem. We have used Cattell's sixteen personality factors (16PF) because, as explained above, they give a good global picture of the individual. We have also measured two other dimensions we thought to be relevant: the level of *innovation* versus *adaptation* shown, and the degree to which the individual shows *type A* or *type B* personality. This last is related to how the individual copes with stress, but all the scales will be discussed fully below.

There is also the issue of how to measure the traits in which we are interested. There are, basically, three possible methods.

1 *Observation.* Watch the individuals in the relevant contexts, and try to assess the degree to which they show the relevant traits. This has the problem of being very subjective, although given the right safeguards it can be effective. We could not use this method anyway, since we were not able to spend time observing the MDs in their work context. We could gain some fairly superficial impressions during the interviews themselves, and we shall, where appropriate, discuss these data, but they must be treated with caution, both because of their subjectivity and because of the 'artificial' nature of the situation. How these MDs related to us as academic researchers could be very different from how they react within the organization.

2 *Self-assessment.* Ask the individuals for their own ratings of themselves. This also has problems of subjectivity and may be biased because the individual is unclear about the precise meaning of the trait. Copeman, for example, asked his sample of chief executives (*The Chief Executive and Business Growth*) whether they saw themselves as introverts or extroverts. This is a very complex and widely misunderstood concept, so, unless it was precisely and clearly defined, considerable bias could arise. In fact, Copeman found that rewording the question produced different responses. Because of these complications, we did not attempt to use this approach.

3 *Tests and questionnaires.* This is also a self-assessment method, where the individual is asked a series of carefully designed and standard questions, which have been thoroughly tested with a large number of people. From the responses given, inferences can be drawn concerning the traits shown by that person. There is a wide popular belief, not without foundation, that responses to these tests can be easily faked. There is also evidence that they produce very accurate pictures of individuals in contexts where there is no reason for faking to occur. As there was no advantage to the individual managing director in faking his response (apart, perhaps, from trying to impress us, and we did not get the impression that any were concerned to do this), tests should give us a reasonably accurate measure. For this reason, this is the method that we used.

Personality

The Personality of the Successful Managing Director

As part of the interview procedure, each managing director was asked if he would complete a number of questionnaires. Not all of them were willing to do so, but about thirty of them did agree. Some were not prepared to do all the tests, so there is some variation in the total number responding in each case.

The Personality Profile

As already indicated, the 16PF was the major measure of personality used, and this was completed by thirty-one of the MDs. It provides scores which can range from 1 to 10 on sixteen major traits. The scoring is arranged so that an average score of 5 to 6 is obtained by about 40 per cent of the population; it then tails off on either side until a score of 1 or 10 is obtained by just over 2 per cent of the general population (see table 8.1). The mean scores obtained on each scale are given in table 8.2, while the distributions are shown in figure 8.2.

The clearest picture is given by figure 8.2. The main feature of this is that the scores are distributed very widely over most of the scales, suggesting that there is no one personality profile indicative of success as a managing director. There is, as might be expected, a strong bias towards being assertive (factor E), all the scores on this scale being 5 or above. There is also a definite tendency towards being *outgoing* (factor A), although there are scores as low as 3 on this scale, showing that some MDs were at the 'reserved' end of the continuum. Factor B (intelligence) is quite interesting in that there are two distinct groups, one group being of average, the other of very high intelligence. It should, however, be admitted that this particular scale is the least reliable in the test. For an accurate measure of intelligence, a more reliable intelligence test is needed. We

TABLE 8.1   Distribution of scores on the 16PF

Score	% of the population
1	2.3
2	4.4
3	9.2
4	15.0
5	19.1
6	19.1
7	15.0
8	9.2
9	4.4
10	2.3

These percentages are obtained by dividing the normal distribution into ten equal intervals. Each division is known as a *standard ten* or *'sten'*.

did not include this, since our assumption was that all the successful individuals in our study would be at the top end of any intelligence scale. This may not be the case. The implication of the result is that it is necessary to be only 'averagely intelligent' to be a managing director, but that many of them are considerably above this level. Two other scales show this tendency to split into two groups. Factor O shows a very wide spread, but with the majority towards the centre, and a clear split between those who are *self-assured* and those who are more *apprehensive*. A similar but less extreme distribution is shown by factor I, with the larger group, perhaps rather surprisingly, being towards the *tender-minded* (sensitive) end of the scale and a smaller group being more *tough-minded* (self-reliant, 'no-nonsense' type).

As already noted, the main feature of the remaining scales is the wide spread of scores obtained. There is, however, a

TABLE 8.2 Mean scores obtained by managing directors on each scale of the 16PF

Factor		Mean score
A	Reserved/Outgoing	6.9
B	Less intelligent/More intelligent	7.0
C	Affected by feelings/emotionally stable	6.7
E	Humble/Assertive	7.1
F	Sober/Happy-go-lucky	4.9
G	Expedient/Conscientious	5.9
H	Shy/Venturesome	5.7
I	Tough-minded/tender-minded	5.8
L	Trusting/Suspicious	4.6
M	Practical/Imaginative	5.9
N	Forthright/Shrewd	6.0
O	Self-assured/Apprehensive	4.5
Q1	Conservative/Experimenting	5.9
Q2	Group-dependent/Self-sufficient	6.6
Q3	Undisciplined/controlled	6.4
Q4	Relaxed/Tense	5.5

N.B. Higher scores indicate that the managing directors have the characteristics represented by the right-hand end of the scale.

slight tendency towards being *emotionally stable* (factor C), *trusting* (factor L), *imaginative* (factor M), *experimenting* (factor Q_1), *self-sufficient* (factor Q_2) and *shrewd* (factor N). Factor Q_3 (undisciplined/controlled) shows quite a wide range of responses, which is perhaps surprising, but with a very slight tendency towards the 'controlled' end of the scale. Another surprise is the very wide range of responses of 'happy-go-lucky'. The implication is that this is perhaps not a particularly discriminating characteristic for success as a managing director. Factor G (expedient/conscientious) and factor H (shy/venturesome) both show a fairly normal distribution, indicating that managing directors are much like the rest of the population on these characteristics. The final scale, factor Q_4 (relaxed/tense), shows a wide range but also tends towards a normal distribution.

High Flyers

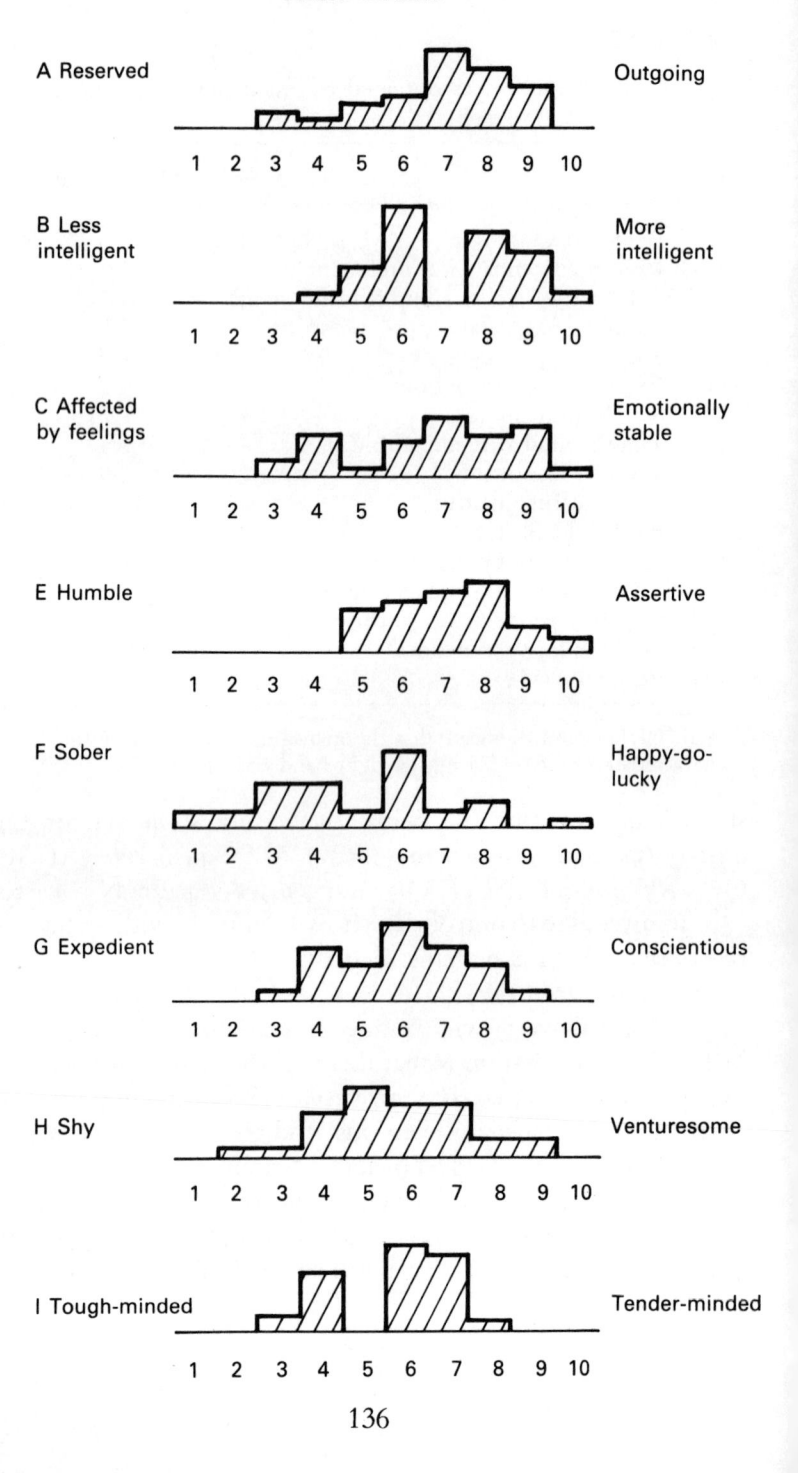

A Reserved — Outgoing
1 2 3 4 5 6 7 8 9 10

B Less intelligent — More intelligent
1 2 3 4 5 6 7 8 9 10

C Affected by feelings — Emotionally stable
1 2 3 4 5 6 7 8 9 10

E Humble — Assertive
1 2 3 4 5 6 7 8 9 10

F Sober — Happy-go-lucky
1 2 3 4 5 6 7 8 9 10

G Expedient — Conscientious
1 2 3 4 5 6 7 8 9 10

H Shy — Venturesome
1 2 3 4 5 6 7 8 9 10

I Tough-minded — Tender-minded
1 2 3 4 5 6 7 8 9 10

PERSONALITY

L Trusting — Suspicious
1 2 3 4 5 6 7 8 9 10

M Practical — Imaginative
1 2 3 4 5 6 7 8 9 10

N Forthright — Shrewd
1 2 3 4 5 6 7 8 9 10

O Self-assured — Apprehensive
1 2 3 4 5 6 7 8 9 10

Q1 Conservative — Experimenting
1 2 3 4 5 6 7 8 9 10

Q2 Group dependent — Self-sufficient
1 2 3 4 5 6 7 8 9 10

Q3 Undisciplined self-conflict — Controlled
1 2 3 4 5 6 7 8 9 10

Q4 Relaxed — Tense
1 2 3 4 5 6 7 8 9 10

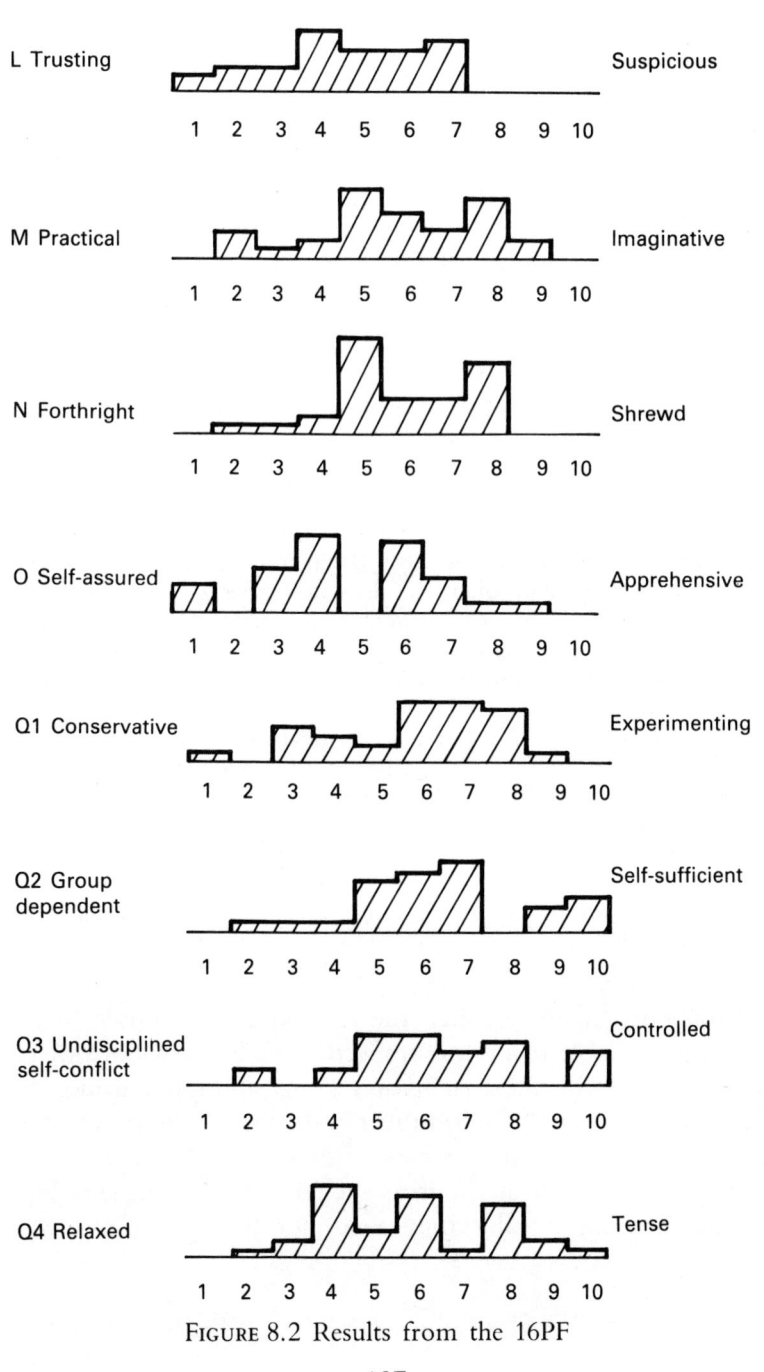

FIGURE 8.2 Results from the 16PF

Adaptors or Innovators

In *Management Initiative*, M.J. Kirton noted two types of managers: those capable of initiating change that improved the current system, but who consistently failed to see possibilities outside the existing system; and 'men of ideas', capable of generating more radical change, but who failed to get their ideas accepted, and so did not succeed in implementing them. He referred to the former as *adaptors* and the latter as *innovators*. In general, 'adaptors' will tend to work within the existing system, while 'innovators' will challenge and change it. Kirton describes the difference in more detail in his 1984 article 'Adaptors and innovators':

> For the marked adaptor, the longer an institutional practice has existed, the more he feels it can be taken for granted. So when confronted by a problem, he does not see it as a stimulus to question or change the structure in which the problem is embedded, but seeks a solution within the structure, in ways already tried and understood—ways which are safe, sure and predictable. He can be relied upon to carry out a thorough, disciplined search for ways to eliminate problems by 'doing things better' with a minimum of risk and a maximum of continuity and stability. This behaviour contrasts strongly with that of the marked innovator. The latter's solution, because it is less understood, and its assumption untested, appears more risky, less sound, involves more 'ripple-effect' changes in areas less obviously needing to be affected; in short, it brings about changes that cannot be envisaged so precisely.

Kirton goes on to say that 'the innovator, in contrast to the adaptor, is liable to be less respectful of the views of others, more abrasive in the presentation of his solution and more at home in a turbulent environment'. 'Adaptors' will more often be found in the more bureaucratic areas of management; 'innovators' tend to be in areas such as research and development. Not unnaturally they tend not to get on too well

Personality

together. 'Adaptors, tend to see 'innovators' as neurotic, as tending to get excited and enthusiastic without cause, and as growing hostile when frustrated in selling their 'revolutionary' ideas. 'Innovators' see 'adaptors' as stodgy, dogmatic, conservative, timid and compliant–as having a strong tendency to agree with their bosses.

The main characteristics of adaptors and innovators

The adaptor	The innovator
Characterized by precision, reliability, efficiency, and conformity.	Tends to be undisciplined and thinks tangentially.
Seeks solutions to problems in tried and understood ways.	Searches for alternative sources for solutions, cutting across current assumptions.
Seen as sound, conforming, safe and dependable.	Often seen as unsound and impractical.
Tends to see the 'means' as the 'goal'	Goes for 'goals' and treats accepted 'means' with little regard.
Is an authority within given structures.	Tends to take control in unstructured situations.
Challenges rules rarely, and then only cautiously, when assured of strong support.	Often challenges rules, has little respect for past custom.
Tends to high self-doubt.	Appears to have low self-doubt.
Essential for the routine functioning of the organization, but occasionally needs to be shaken out of his systematic approach.	Is ideal in unforeseen crises, and in helping to avoid them, but may need controlling from time to time.

As with other aspects of personality, people are not necessarily at one or other extreme, but can be placed along a continuum with the extremes at either end. According to Kirton, where an individual is placed on this continuum depends on the balance of three factors. The degree of *originality*, *efficiency* (i.e. the extent to which the person is precise and disciplined) and his or her *rule/group conformity* (i.e. the extent to which the individual is constrained by rules or the norms of his group). An 'adaptor' can be quite original (or creative), but will also be high on efficiency (i.e. methodical and precise) and something of a conformist, so that his or her creativity is confined within the system. The 'innovator', high on originality but low on conformity and efficiency, will be much less confined by traditional approaches to problems, and so will be more likely to challenge the existing system. The Kirton Adaptation–Innovation Inventory (KAI), which measures a person's position on this continuum, is arranged so that a high score indicates an innovator and a low score an adaptor.

Only twenty-six of the managing directors in our study completed the KAI. This was partly because the format of the questionnaire is slightly unusual. Respondents are asked to rate themselves on how 'easy or difficult' they find it to *present themselves*, consistently, over a long period on a series of thirty-three items. These include, for example, rating yourself on how easy it would be to present yourself as 'a person who is patient'. Ratings are made on a five-point scale from 'very hard' to 'very easy'. Respondents seemed to find this harder than rating how they actually are. One MD commented that the problem was that he could easily present himself in any way asked. However, despite these difficulties, the results are interesting.

Table 8.3 shows the distribution of the scores obtained on the KAI by the twenty-six MDs and compares them with those obtained by the general population. All the MDs are in the top half of the distribution, indicating that they are 'innovators' rather than 'adaptors': 54 per cent are in the top 20 per cent for the whole population, indicating that they are strongly on the innovator end of the scale; 34 per cent are moderate innovators—just above the halfway mark. The implication is that managing directors do not get to their positions by following the rules and accepting authority. They are more likely to challenge the existing system and find novel solutions to problems. In fact, managers in general do score slightly higher (more innovative) than the general population, but the difference is not statistically significant. These MDs are therefore significantly more innovative than most managers. This challenges the myth that the way to the top is to 'toe the line' and not to 'make waves'. From the evidence of our interviews, these MDs were not, in any case, the sort of people to take this latter course.

TABLE 8.3 Scores obtained by managing directors on the Kirton Innovation–Adaptation questionnaire

Score	No. in sample	% in sample	% in total population
119+	6	23	10
111–118	8	31	10
105–110	3	12	10
101–104	4	15	10
95–103	5	19	10
Total	26	100	50

Type A/B Personality

The concept of *type A* and *type B* personality was developed by M. Friedman and R.H. Rosenman during a study of patients with coronary heart disease (In Rosenman, Friedman and Strauss, 'CHD in the Western collaborative group study'). It was found that the coronary patients under study behaved similarly in many ways: they were extremely competitive, high-achieving, aggressive, hasty, impatient and restless. They were characterized by explosive speech patterns, tenseness of facial muscles and appearing to be under time pressure. These individuals were described as 'type A' personality types as opposed to the more relaxed 'type Bs', who had low risks of coronary heart disease. Type As have been described as people so deeply involved and committed to their work that other aspects of their lives are relatively neglected.

Type A/B behaviour patterns

The original type A theorists, Friedman and Rosenman, identified type A characteristics in their book, *Type A Behaviour and Your Heart*. They outline the following characteristics of type A personality:

1 Possessing the habit of explosively accentuating various key words in ordinary speech without real need and tending to utter the last few words of sentences far more rapidly than the opening words. Friedman and Rosenman believe the first habit reflects underlying aggression or hostility, while the second 'mirrors your underlying impatience with spending even the time required for your own speech'.
2 Always moving, walking and eating rapidly.
3 Feeling or revealing to others an 'impatience with the rate at which most events take place.' Finding it 'difficult to restrain from hurrying the speech of others and resorting to the device of saying very quickly, over and over again, "uh huh, uh huh", or saying "yes yes, yes yes", to someone who is talking', urging him to hurry up. Often finishing the sentences of persons speaking.
4 Often attempting to do two or more things at the same time, such as thinking about an irrelevant subject when listening to someone else speak. 'Similarly, if while golfing or fishing you continue to ponder business or professional problems or while using an electric razor you attempt also to eat your breakfast or drive your car or if while driving your car you attempt to dictate letters for your secretary'. Rosenman and Friedman describe this 'polyphasic' activity as one of the most common traits of the type A individual.
5 Finding it difficult to refrain from talking about or turning any conversation to themes which have personal interest.

At times when this manoevre fails, pretending to listen but really remaining preoccupied with these personal thoughts.
6. Almost always feeling vaguely guilty when attempting to relax or do nothing for even just a few hours.
7. No longer noticing the more interesting or lovely things encountered during the day.
8. Not having 'any time to spare to become the things worth being because you are so preoccupied with getting the things worth having.'
9. Attempting to 'schedule more and more in less and less time'. Making fewer allowances for unforeseen events which might disrupt the schedule. Also having a 'chronic sense of time urgency'–a core aspect of the type A personality.
10. On meeting another severely afflicted type A person, instead of feeling compassion for his affliction you find yourself compelled to 'challenge' him. This is a telltale trait because no one arouses the agressive and/or hostile feelings of one type A subject more quickly than another type A subject.
11. Resorting to 'certain characteristic gestures or nervous tics' such as clenching fists, banging a hand upon a table for emphasis.
12. Becoming increasingly committed to translating and evaluating personal activities and the activities of others in terms of 'numbers'.

Rosenman and Friedman also outline the following characteristics as indicating the type B personality:

1. Being 'completely free of all of the habits and exhibiting none of the traits of the type A personality.'
2. Never suffering from time urgency and impatience.
3. Harbouring no 'free-floating hostility' and feeling no need to impress others with your achievements or accomplishments unless the situation demands it.
4. Playing in order to find relaxation and fun, not to demonstrate achievement at any cost.
5. Being able to work without agitation, 'relax without guilt'.

Many other studies have confirmed the relationship between coronary heart disease and type A behaviour. Type A men have been found to have a number of symptoms or risk factors of heart disease such as raised blood pressure and high cholesterol levels. Other researchers have attempted to see if there is a link between type A behaviour and stress indicators. In general, no significant correlations have been found between type A behaviour and various stress measures such as job dissatisfaction, sleeping disorders, anxiety, depression, irritation and physical 'stress'. The researchers found instead that type A behaviour acted as an intervening factor: when type A behaviour was combined with work and family stressors it predicted stress-related illness. Other studies have indicated that type A behaviour may lie dormant until the individual is faced with a challenging, stressful situation; at that time, the combination of type A behaviour and an extensive stressor may combine to trigger a physical reaction such as a heart attack.

In addition, a link between high-status jobs and type A behaviour has been indicated. One study looked at 943 white-collar, middle-class males in Buffalo, New York. The men came from five different work settings–administrative and professional staff of a state health agency; supervisory personnel from a public-service organization; officers from trade unions; faculty staff from a major private university; and administrative officers from a large banking corporation. Not only was the type A behaviour pattern related to occupational status as measured by rank, level of occupational prestige and income; it was also found to be significantly related to rapid career achievement as indicated by rank and income relative to age. A review of a number of studies bears out the connection between type A personality and high occupational status. Type As tend to describe their jobs as having more responsibility, longer hours and heavier workloads than do type Bs. Despite these factors, type As in general do not report more job disatisfaction, anxiety or depression than do type Bs. Against this background, it seemed very relevant to measure the type A or type B behaviour of the managing directors in our study.

The Type A/B Behaviour Questionnaire

The Type A/B Behaviour Questionnaire was formulated by R.W. Bortner ('A short rating scale as potential measure of pattern A behaviour'). The type A personality is characterized as hard-driving, involved in work, persistent, aggressive, having a heightened sense of time urgency, and being oriented towards leadership and achievement. Type B personality characterics, by contrast, tend towards the opposite attributes. The questionnaire consists of fourteen bipolar scales representing these two trends in personality and behaviour. Respondents are asked to assess the extent to which they possess such behavioural patterns, using an 11-point rating system. The type A/B behaviour scores can be divided into four categories: type A1, type A2, type B1, type B2. The people with the highest scores are type A1 and with the lowest type B2. In the general population, type A1s usually represent 10 per cent, type A2s 40 per cent, type B1s 40 per cent and type B2s 10 per cent.

Table 8.4 gives a summary of the results from the Type A/B Behaviour Questionnaire which was completed by thirty managing directors. The results are highly significant: 57 per cent are type A1, of which there are only 10 per cent in the general population; 90 per cent are in the top half of the distribution and are thus classified as either type A1 or A2, equivalent to 50 per cent of the general population. The data in this case confirm the popular mythology of the businessman at risk of heart attacks and other stress-related illnesses. It is also consistent with their fairly frenetic lifestyle discussed in chapter 4. We did not ask questions specifically on medical history, although had we known the above data in advance we might well have done, but despite these scores our impression is that all the MDs in the group were particularly healthy. Many do have regular medical check-ups, and virtually all were involved in moderately energetic spare-time activities–golf, walking, game fishing and shooting being the most popular. As also mentioned earlier, the vast majority had

Type A/B Behaviour Questionnaire

Please circle one number for each of the 14 questions below, which best reflects the way you behave in your everyday life.

For example, if you are always on time for appointments, on question 1 you would circle a number between 7 and 11. If you are usually more casual about appointments you would circle one of the lower numbers between 1 and 5.

Casual about appointments	1 2 3 4 5 6 7 8 9 10 11	Never late
Not competitive	1 2 3 4 5 6 7 8 9 10 11	Very competitive
Good listener	1 2 3 4 5 6 7 8 9 10 11	Anticipates what others are going to say (nods, attempts to finish for them)
Never feels rushed (even under pressure)	1 2 3 4 5 6 7 8 9 10 11	Always rushed
Can wait patiently	1 2 3 4 5 6 7 8 9 10 11	Impatient while waiting
Takes things one at a time	1 2 3 4 5 6 7 8 9 10 11	Tries to do many things at once, thinks about what will do next
Slow deliberate talker	1 2 3 4 5 6 7 8 9 10 11	Emphatic in speech, fast and forceful
Cares about satisfying him/herself no matter what others may think	1 2 3 4 5 6 7 8 9 10 11	Wants good job, recognized by others

PERSONALITY

Slow doing things	1 2 3 4 5 6 7 8 9 10 11	Fast (eating, walking)
Easy going	1 2 3 4 5 6 7 8 9 10 11	Hard-driving (pushing yourself and others)
Expresses feelings	1 2 3 4 5 6 7 8 9 10 11	Hides feelings
Many outside interests	1 2 3 4 5 6 7 8 9 10 11	Few interests outside work/home
Unambitious	1 2 3 4 5 6 7 8 9 10 11	Ambitious
Casual	1 2 3 4 5 6 7 8 9 10 11	Eager to get things done

Lowest type B score = 14 Highest type A score = 154
High type A behaviour = 95+ Vulnerable type A behaviour = 120+
Average score = 84

very supportive wives and family lives. It would seem then, that, despite apparently being at very high risk of stress-related illness, these successful MDs had developed good coping strategies and were in practice no (or not much) more at risk than the rest of us.

It is also interesting to look at the distribution of responses on each item of the Type A/B Behaviour Questionnaire. These are shown in figure 8.3. There are six scales where there is a strong tendency for the responses to cluster at one end. Thus most of these MDs are 'never late', 'very competitive', 'go all out', are 'fast at eating, walking, etc.' 'hard-driving' and 'ambitious'. These are all clear type A characteristics. They also tend towards 'emphatic speech' and 'doing many things at once' but are 'never rushed'. They also tend towards

TABLE 8..4 Scores obtained by managing directors on the Type A/B Behaviour Questionnaire

	no. in sample	% in sample	% in total population
Type A1 score 104–140	17	57	10
Type A2 score 91–103	10	33	40
Type B3 score 65–90	3	10	40
Type B4 score 10–64	0	0	10
Total	30	100	100

'impatience', although there is quite a wide spread on this scale. On the four remaining scales the responses are very evenly spread. This is particularly true of the scale 'wants good job recognized by others' versus 'cares about satisfying himself'. This would indicate that this is not a relevant characteristic for managing directors, which is at odds with the emphasis on intrinsic motivation which emerged from the interviews. There is a similarly wide spread on 'expressing feelings', which is consistent with the general taboo on the expression of feelings which is common in most organizations. We wonder in fact, for those who do 'express feelings', to what extent it is *negative* rather than positive feelings which are revealed.

Managing directors also differ widely on how well they *think* they listen, this scale tending towards the bimodal – that is respondents are either good or bad listeners, with few in the middle. This conforms with our experience during the interviews, but in view of the commitment to open and consultative management it is an important skill. The scale relating to the extent of outside interests is even more clearly bimodal. Chief executives tend to fall into two categories, those with outside interests and those without. This is slightly at odds with the data from the interviews, where we were struck by the lack of outside interests reported, apart from the outdoor activities already mentioned, and by the long hours worked. What many MDs have recorded as outside interests is membership of committees of such bodies as trade associations and the CBI. We would not see these as truly outside activities, but as all part of the very busy, work-directed life of the average MD.

Observations from the Interviews

The impressions that we gained from the interviews correspond very closely with the data from the 16PF. These managing directors certainly came over to us as highly self-confident and assertive. Their social skills are also highly developed so that the impact was very positive. Although quite dominant, they did not appear domineering, and our interaction with them was, in all cases, a very pleasant experience. There were, however, a number of additional facets of personality which were evident both from how they behaved and from what they said about themselves. The main facet is that they have a very high *internal locus of control*. By this is meant that they work from internal reference-points and are influenced in their actions mainly by their own internal beliefs and values, not by reference to what others think should be done. This is linked to their self-confidence, which arises from their strong internal value system, and it also means they take responsibility for their own actions, since they see themselves as 'self-controlled' rather than 'controlled by others'.

We also came away with the impression of having met a group of people with very high levels of 'determination'. This is shown by their ability to set very clear objectives, to some extent for themselves, but more particularly for their

HIGH FLYERS

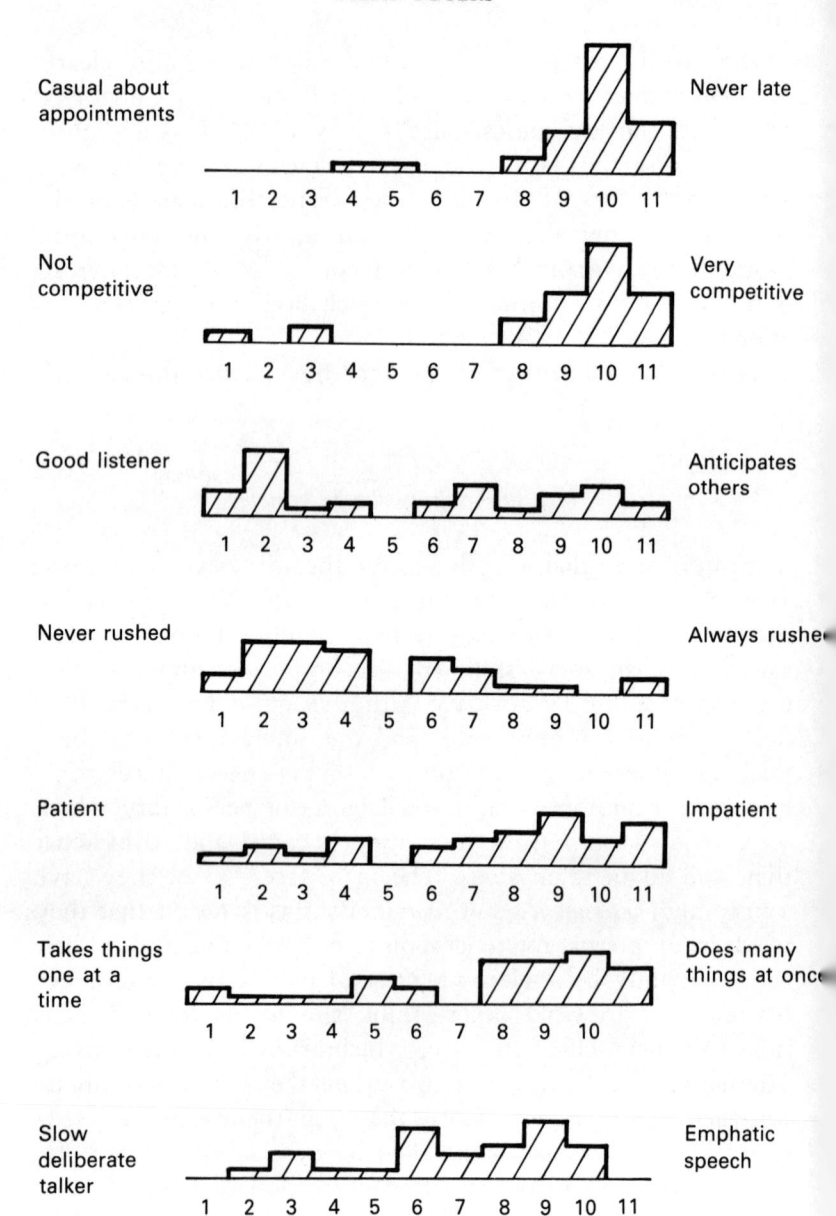

Casual about appointments — Never late

Not competitive — Very competitive

Good listener — Anticipates others

Never rushed — Always rushed

Patient — Impatient

Takes things one at a time — Does many things at once

Slow deliberate talker — Emphatic speech

PERSONALITY

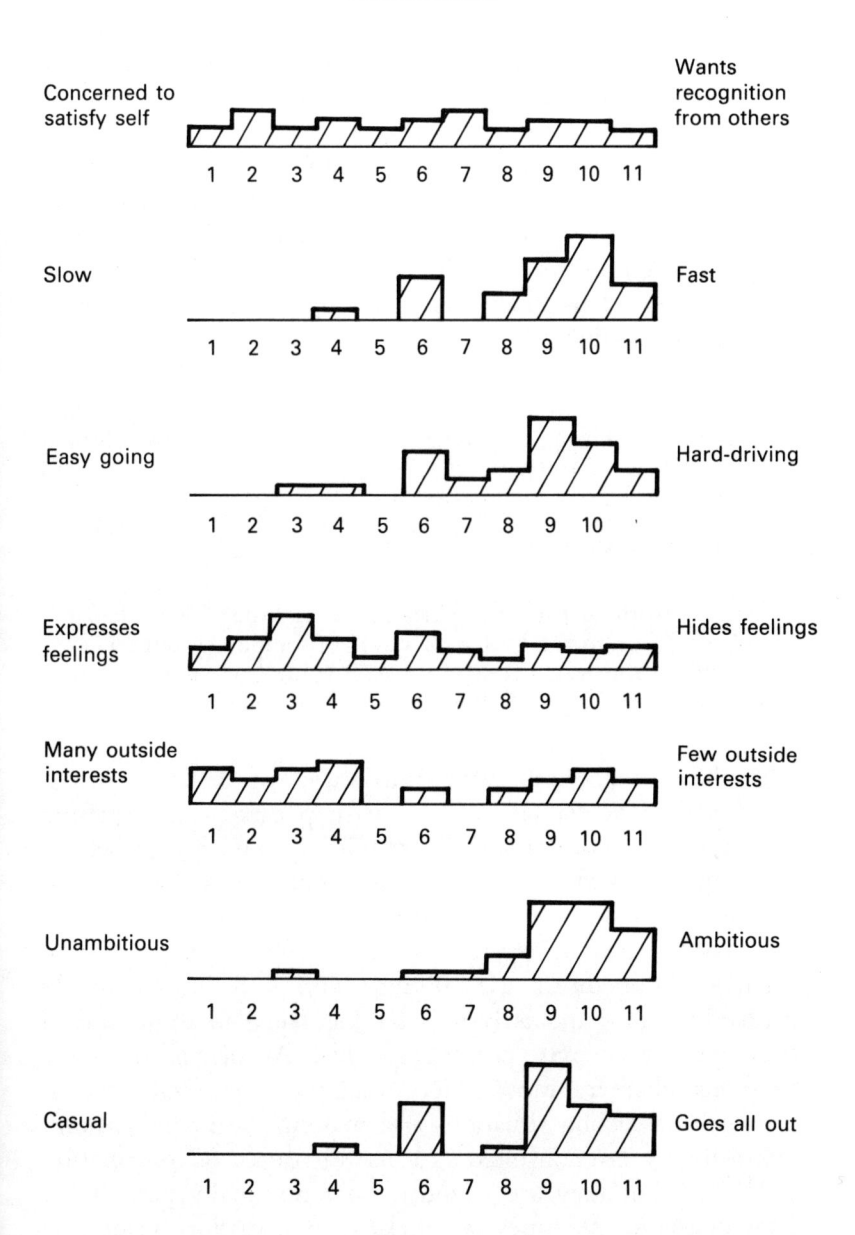

Concerned to satisfy self		Wants recognition from others
	1 2 3 4 5 6 7 8 9 10 11	
Slow		Fast
	1 2 3 4 5 6 7 8 9 10 11	
Easy going		Hard-driving
	1 2 3 4 5 6 7 8 9 10	
Expresses feelings		Hides feelings
	1 2 3 4 5 6 7 8 9 10 11	
Many outside interests		Few outside interests
	1 2 3 4 5 6 7 8 9 10 11	
Unambitious		Ambitious
	1 2 3 4 5 6 7 8 9 10 11	
Casual		Goes all out
	1 2 3 4 5 6 7 8 9 10 11	

FIGURE 8.3 Results from the Type A/B Behaviour Questionnaire

organizations, and then to follow through to see them achieved. An important aspect of this is the ability to *cope with adversity* – to learn from it rather than being discouraged. Most had shown an ability to bounce back from negative situations at some stage in their career. They also have the ability to cope with any unpleasant aspects involved in achieving objectives, most marked in recent years by dealing with redundancy programmes. This quality is illustrated by the comment of one managing director:

> It is surprising how easily many people seem to accept defeat, and I think not being prepared to be beaten (a sort of stickability) can carry you through a hell of a long way.

He later went on to say:

> The competitive part is important. I hate losing, and when I do lose I like to think of it as a sort of temporary setback–as a battle in the war; that you can still come back and win the war. I don't like people beating me at anything.

The third impression we gained was of a fairly strong underlying *authoritarian* streak. This is perhaps not surprising if you are a self-confident person with a strong set of beliefs. We emphasize *underlying*, because this trait does not seem to be manifested in outright autocratic behaviour. Because of their social skills, most successful MDs can bring people along with them without direct use of authority, and indeed would probably regard themselves as having failed in some way if they were unable to accomplish this. As discussed in the previous chapter, most chief executives see their role as primarily 'assessing situations and making the final decision'. Subordinates are consulted as a useful source of information and ideas, but they are at most, only nominally part of the final decision. At times we picked up a distinct pride and pleasure that these MDs took in their ability to get their own way.

Powerful Personalities

J.M. Close, quoting several other sources in his article 'Dogmatism and managerial achievement', lists the characteristics of successful managers as being high on personal adjustment, self-assurance, initiative, dominance, confidence and straightforwardness, while they are low on emotionality, anxiety and autonomy. They demonstrate greater intelligence than both the general population and less successful managers and have high aspirations and desire for responsibility. He also found top managers to be less dogmatic than those more junior. R. Spillane, in *Achieving Peak Performance*, suggests that effective managers show self-assurance, decisiveness, intelligence, independence and risk-taking. McCall and Lombardo list among the reasons for success of the executives in their study of successful versius 'derailed' executives, *Off the Track*, that they were outgoing, well liked, charming and technically brilliant. The 'fatal flaws' of those executives who became 'derailed' include insensitivity to others; an abrasive, intimidating, bullying style; and being cold, aloof and arrogant. All of these findings are broadly consistent with our own. Charles Garfield, in his study of *Peak Performers*, makes three key points which are totally in line with our results. First, the primary locus of control for a peak performer in business is 'internal'. Secondly, they are high in *self mastery*, an important element of which is *self-confidence*, which he describes as follows:

> Self-confidence stems from the feeling, and the evidence to back it up, that you know what you are doing and do it well. You can see the arguments for and against any decision, but you do not hesitate to make the decision and to live with it.
>
> Self-confident people feel an internal authority to act, based on a sense of their own expertise and the knowledge that if something goes awry they will know what to do. They count on their capabilities being equal to the task. In short, they trust their own effectiveness.

Self-confidence is internal mastery. Effectiveness is external mastery. Each supports the other.

The third characteristic he calls *ego strength*, which is similar to *hardiness*:

> Ego strength often shows up in business and elsewhere as hardiness – the energy to sustain long hours of work and the flexibility to adapt to change. Hardiness comes from a strong sense of being on course. Less confident co-workers spend significant amounts of their energy hiding behind pronouncements of policy and 'higher authority' and manoevring to protect their skins, which tend to be thin.

Our findings from the 16PF show that chief executives are 'assertive' and 'outgoing'. The type A/B questionnaire showed them to be competitive, hard-driving, ambitious and time-conscious. They are 'innovators' rather than 'adaptors', and came over in the interviews as 'self-confident', 'internally controlled' and 'determined'. Less clearly defined is a tendency to be emotionally stable, trusting, imaginative, expedient and shrewd. All of this adds up to a pretty powerful personality. There are no very great surprises in this picture. Perhaps the stereotype of the big-business executive would not include a trusting or imaginative nature. But if you are confident and sure of yourself you can afford to be trusting; in addition, it must take imagination to guide and develop a large enterprise. These characteristics, anyway, are balanced by a degree of expediency and shrewdness.

Summary

The managing directors in this study showed very varied personalities but with some key traits in common. It is not really very surprising that chief executives of large companies have powerful personalities and are *assertive* and *outgoing*. They also tend to be *emotionally stable, trusting, imaginative,*

> Men and women of entirely different personalities can and do become successful executives. There are, however, a number of traits common to such people. I would expect to find ambition, judgement, a desire for responsibility, an ability to make decisions quickly, determination, application, persistence, a preparedness to take risks, an ability to delegate, an understanding of what motivates others, a recognition that detail does matter, a sense of humour, health, a patient spouse and the knowledge that 'It can be done'.
> (Lord Hanson, Chairman, The Hanson Trust)

experimenting, self-sufficient and *shrewd*. They are very *innovative*; that is, they are prepared, if necessary, to challenge and change the existing system and not be constrained by conventional assumptions and beliefs. This characteristic stems from having a high *internal locus of control* and *self-confidence*, coupled with *originality* and *low conformity*, when occasion demands, to rules and group norms. They score very highly on type A behaviour, showing themselves to be *hard driving, aggressive, time-conscious* and *heavily involved in work*. This puts them at risk from coronary heart disease and other stress-related illnesses, but their attention to their own health and their generally healthy lifestyle outside working hours probably mitigate the worst effects of this aspect of their lives. Life is not always smooth for the 'top man' in any organization, and chief executives develop effective strategies for coping with adversity – treating setbacks as challenges to be overcome and opportunities for learning. All in all, theirs is a very positive approach to life.

9
THE ANATOMY OF MANAGERIAL SUCCESS

In this final chapter we shall bring together all the information that we have concerning the attributes and background of the successful top-level manager, with the intention of building a picture of the successful 'high flyer'. As we said in chapter 1, there are two main aims in doing this. One is to provide information to aid the processes of selection and development of chief executives and other top managers. The other is to provide some guidelines for individuals in their own development. This is apart from the sheer intrinsic interest of knowing what the 'managers at the top' of our major organizations are really like.

CHARACTERISTICS OF THE SUCCESSFUL CHIEF EXECUTIVE

The group of highly successful managing directors who form the basis of this study have a number of personal characteristics in common, which are certainly related to their success. While it may be possible to operate successfully at the top level without one or more of these, it clearly makes success more probable if all are present. Obviously not all of the MDs did have all the characteristics, and it may be that one method used to enable them to succeed was to select other members of the top team with compensating abilities. This makes it all the more important to know which characteristics are important and which of these one does, or does not, possess. These key characteristics are as follows.

Determination These successful managers were all very determined and quite assertive individuals. This came through very clearly in the interviews and was reflected in the data from the 16PF questionnaire. This may well be a characteristic derived from their early experience, which for many of them involved situations (e.g. separation from their parents when very young) which required them to take responsibility for themselves at quite an early stage in their lives. When thrown on their resources while still very young, they needed quite a bit of determination to survive. If the individual succeeds, it may well set a pattern for later life.

Learning from adversity Most MDs had experienced setbacks and problems during their careers, but had taken advantage of these as 'opportunities' for learning and development. Some, indeed, had knowingly taken on difficult jobs, partly for the challenge but also for the opportunities presented. Others had simply been 'thrown in at the deep end', finding themselves coping with situations which they had not anticipated. The common characteristic is that they survived and coped very successfully, learning a great deal in the process. This characteristic probably also derives from their early experience and is related to their determination.

Seizing chances when presented All the MDs in our study were highly proactive and would respond to challenge. Most had been offered the opportunity of high levels of responsibility at a relatively early age and had taken this opportunity with enthusiasm. Often the challenges were quite daunting, such as taking over an ailing subsidiary or coping with an overseas operation in a strange culture far away from head-office support and encouragement.

Achievement Orientation They were all ambitious people with a need to achieve, but not in the rather narrow sense used by

McClelland. They measured their success not by 'winning small battles' but by long-term achievement. They were also more concerned with the overall success of the organization than with short-term career aims. Related to this was a very *positive* approach to life. They were motivated very much by 'hope of success' rather than 'fear of failure'.

Internal locus of control Part of their very positive approach to life was due to their high level of self-confidence, which in turn derived from clear 'internal reference-points', which were used to guide action. They had a very clear *internal* map of how the world is and ought to be. This facilitated positive action without self-doubt.

Well-integrated value system Most of the chief executives interviewed had a clear set of values, which were well articulated. A key value was *integrity*, which implies being dependable and doing what you say you will do. Other values underpinned many of the points made above. They include the valuing of *achievement, independence* and *intitiative*, but emphasis was also placed on *people and relationships*, which was felt to be important for individuals whose success is measured in organizational terms.

Effective management of risk Successful MDs were not high risk-takers; this seems to be more a characteristic of the entrepreneur. The MDs in this study saw themselves as 'moderate risk-takers', and this fits with the evidence. Most had taken some risk, both at a personal level in, for example, career decisions, and at an organizational level in decisions taken in their job. The important element is that they were sure that they had the skills to cope with the situation they were entering, and so did not see it as particularly risky. In most instances, they appear to have been right.

Clear objectives The successful MD knows where he is going. This is true at both the personal and the organizational level.

They universally stressed the need to be clear about the long-term objectives of the organization, and the need to have the determination to achieve them. At the personal level, goals were rather short-term and mainly concerned with doing the current job well. Most MDs, perhaps unexpectedly, denied having specific long-term career goals. The belief was that, if you do well at what you are doing in the present, the future takes care of itself. There seems an inherent contradiction here: if organizational success depends on clarity and determination in relation to long-term goals, why should personal success be any different?

High dedication to the job All the CEOs in this study worked very long hours and clearly regarded their job as by far the most important element of their lives, with the possible exception of their families. For a minority, even the family came second. Clearly, much of their personal fulfillment and confirmation of their worth as human beings came from their work.

Intrinsic motivation This is a corollary of their dedication to the job. If work is not intrinsically motivating, it is impossible to be dedicated to it. All the MDs in the study found their work completely 'involving and enjoyable'. One of the strongest impressions we gained concerned the universal *energy* and *enthusiasm* engendered by work.

Well-organized life We found very little evidence of serious conflict between work and home life. This is mainly because they were well organized and used their time effectively both at work and at home. It must, however, also be admitted that this was because work nearly always took precedence. The wife looked after and organized the home and coped with her husband's 'unavoidable' absences due to the demands of work.

Pragmatic approach The approach to life of the successful top manager is essentially pragmatic, not intellectual. This shows

I have to believe that your research into chief executives' requirements in their senior executives is going to leave you sifting through one of the largest collections of motherhood statements ever issued by our 'captains of industry'. However, for myself I seek:

1	*Raw Intellect* comprising IQ, numeracy, speed of response, verbal ability, logic	Tested by whatever methods are preferred by the line managers concerned, so long as the methods are well validated.
2	*Forthright Honesty*	Difficult to determine and best done by third-party reference and interview.
3	*Determination* (not ambition)	Lengthy interview, group selection and track record are good but far from infallible guides.
4	*Physical Durability*	Reject the fat men, the heavy smokers, the obvious drinkers and the medically suspect. Sheer prejudice but good risk aversion
5	*Is he a shit?*	If yes, reject him: more prejudice, but in the end why work with too many people you don't like? Usually you inherit more than enough—why hire more?
6	*Personality Profile*	Again tested by whatever methods you like so long as validation is sound. Not highest on my list of assessment criteria but a *sine qua non*. Avoid true hedonists as totally as true Calvinists. Flamboyance of itself, however, is no bad thing.

The Anatomy of Managerial Success

7 (and most importantly) *Track Record*	If the man has done a similar job successfully (and for a sufficiently long period) give him the benefit of the doubt on all the other criteria unless cumulatively they are in your highly personal view overwhelmingly negative.

(Sir James Blyth, Managing Director, The Plessey Company plc)

very clearly in spare-time activities, which were almost entirely 'practical'. Very few individuals mentioned intellectual interests or pursuits.

Sound analytic and problem-solving skills Time and time again MDs emphasized the importance of being able to analyse a problem and reach an effective solution. This was seen as an absolutely fundamental skill. This does not seem to be a highly intellectual process, but is rather the ability to recognize the factors involved and 'see the wood for the trees'. Quite often this would be 'intuitive' rather than strictly rational.

> Intellectual ability and breadth of experience to identify strategic direction–to act for the corporate good rather than for a particular function or division.
>
> The social expertise to manage external relationships, whether political, customer, shareholder or supplier, at the highest level and in different organizational and national cultures.
>
> The leadership skills to lead and build teams, to lead both the corporation and its specific parts. The ability to act also as a member of a team.
>
> The flexibility and patience to cope with the hectic pace and fragmented activities normal in a top executive role–not only dealing with man issues at once but recognizing the order of their importance and their relationship one to the other.
>
> Numeracy to help formulate financial policy and to cope with the increasing need to understand complex financial statements.
>
> Commerical intuition–while formal analytical skills are important, a strong commercial 'sense' is more valuable.
>
> (Anthony R. Pilkington Chairman Pilkington plc)

High level of 'people skills' Since all top managers, by definition achieve their organizational objectives through other people, it follows that, to be successful, they must have a high level of interpersonal skills. Most MDs seem to operate an open and consultative style, but with a strong authoritarian back-up. However, whatever the style–from authoritarian to participative–the skills required are the same. These include the ability to select appropriate team members in the first place, communication skills, and the maintenance of motivation.

High level of innovation All the MDs who completed the Kirton Adaptation–Innovation Inventory were in the upper half of the distribution, i.e. they were 'innovators' rather than 'adaptors', some of them very strongly so. In other words, they were the sort of people who in making changes would not be constrained by the existing system, but would challenge existing procedures and assumptions, thus producing something *new* rather than modification of what currently exists. This is a very important characteristic for someone who is responsible the long-term development of a large organization.

Type A personality The results of the Type A/B Behaviour Questionnaire showed very strong trends towards type A personality, which comprises a very aggressive, high-achieving, competitive and hard-driving lifestyle. The energy involved in this type of behaviour undoubtedly contributes to success, but it may be at a price. High type As are prone to coronary heart disease and other stress-related illnesses. However, an attempt to *manage* the extremes of this behaviour, and to promote healthy living to some extent, may mitigate the worst effects of this lifestyle.

> We have recently carried out a study in British Steel into the abilities which are required in future top managers in this industry. We have used this work, which was written up in the *Institute of Management Studies Journal* in Spring 1987, to guide us in the kind of preparation individuals approaching

The Anatomy of Managerial Success

these jobs require. Broadly this study suggested the following major abilities:

1 *Ability to diagnose problems.* This includes the ability to assimilate complicated information against a changing environment, to analyse it and organize it and to think the issues through. Effective individuals explore figures and information presented to them, challenge and ask questions about it and are not overawed by technical presentations.
2 *An ability to identify, prioritize and solve problems.* Successful managers use their staff to help identify problems earlier rather than later, manage the initiatives taken from within the team responsible for them, take sound judgements on the risks involved in order to capitalize on opportunities. They steer a sensible course between being over-cautious on the one hand and taking snap decisions on the other.
3 *Managing change.* Effective business heads have a forward vision of where their business will be over the next five to ten years. They respond to a changing environment and have the commitment and energy to define major change needs. They have the overall capacity to develop a broad strategy, taking into consideration a wide variety of business aspects.
4 *The management of human resource.* Our most effective managers provide firm, clear and agreed controls for their management teams. They are visible and seen to be in control. They operate in a team spirit as well as being effective leaders; they avoid paternalism and the autocratic style.
5 *Business awareness.* An understanding of the commerical and financial aspects of the world at large is essential for business managers today. They must have a clear understanding of their markets and an appreciation of the financial management of their business. They must be able to deal with technical matters, and they must have an international perspective rather than being parochial or limited in their approach.
6 *Personal qualities.* Finally, the personal qualities of managers are, of course, paramount. Effective managers have a high level of commitment, they demonstrate this, and they are able to tolerate high levels of stress in their work. They are also good communicators who understand the importance of getting across simple messages in an easily understandable form to ordinary people in the workplace.
(Sir Robert Scholey, Chairman, British Steel Corporation)

A Developmental Model for Managerial Success

It is very clear that there are a number of characteristics which highly successful managers tend to have in common. Some of these are to do with their early childhood and career experience. Other factors which are shared by most successful top executives are concerned with personality. Many of these traits will have been determined, to some degree, by their experience. While it is impossible to say to what extent any particular aspect of personality is a product of heredity or environment, it is obvious that experience plays a very large part in the development of these characteristics. A third area of importance is the behaviour shown by successful managers–what do they *actually do* that makes them successful, and what, apart from their personality, determines this behaviour? It is possible to organize these factors into a three-stage model as outlined in figure 9.1. The centre of this is the successful *individual personality*. This is strongly influenced by a variety of *developmental experiences*, and in turn will influence *effective managerial performance*. Each of these areas will be discussed in turn, starting with the successful personality.

Developmental experiences → Individual personality → Determinants of performance

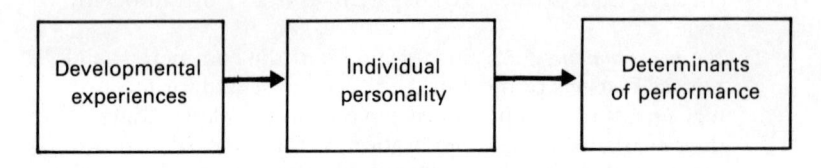

FIGURE 9.1 Three aspects of the development of the high flyer

The Personality of the High Flyer

In looking for a way in which to summarize and encapsulate the successful managerial personality, we hit upon the idea of using the concept of *structural analysis* from Berne's theory of *transactional analysis*. This is, in effect, a structured personality

The Anatomy of Managerial Success

theory. Briefly, Berne suggested that we could view the individual as having three main ways of *being* or of responding to the world. These are known as *ego states*.

The Parent ego state is concerned with values and standards. It is the repository of all our beliefs about how we and others should behave. Since our values determine whether we are critical, controlling or nurturing, the Parent is the source of these behaviours. A review of the previous section will show that the successful managing director has a well-developed Parent. We noted their 'well-developed value system' and their tendency towards being 'controlling' in relation to their subordinates. Interestingly, there was no overall evidence of a strong Nurturing Parent. Although this was undoubtedly present in some individuals, it does not seem to be a necessary (as opposed to sufficient) condition for success in management.

The Adult ego state is concerned with logic and rational thinking. It is obvious that this is a very strong characteristic of all the MDs in this study. They all emphasized the importance of 'logical analysis and problem-solving' ability. The setting of objectives, while partly determined by values, also has a very strong rational element. One requires logical thought to test the reality and feasibility of an objective, to check that it is consistent with other objectives, with legal requirements and with other external constraints. The effective management of risk also requires the rational analysis of the probable outcomes of different courses of action, and the costs and consequences of actions going wrong.

The Child ego state is concerned with feelings. It is the source of energy as well as intuition and creativity. Again the data show that successful chief executives have a well-developed Child. This is shown, particularly, by the enormous energy and enthusiasm they have for their jobs. High creativity is implied by their innovative approach, and many MDs stressed that problem-solving is an intuitive process as well as a rational one. We did not find much evidence in the data we collected of Adapted Child. Managing directors do not seem to be particularly *compliant* or *rebellious,* and, indeed, any marked

Structural analysis

Structural analysis is a core part of *transactional analysis* (TA), which is a set of related constructs that describe personality structure and its behavioural manifestations. TA is particularly concerned with how people relate to one another.

Structural analysis is based on the concept of *ego states*. An *ego state* has been defined as a 'consistent pattern of feelings and experiences directly related to a corresponding consistent pattern of behaviour'. It is a way of *being*. Each person has three ego states, or groups of feelings, experiences and behaviours, namely, *Parent ego state*, *Adult ego state* and *Child ego state*. When referring to an ego state, the name is capitalized to distinguish it from the normal use of the word. While there is an obvious connection with the everyday use of the words 'parent', 'adult', and 'child', it is important to note that their meaning is not the same. They are used in TA as specially defined technical terms. For example, to refer to someone as 'coming from' (or behaving from) their Child does not have the same meaning as calling them 'childish'.

The *Child ego state* is derived from childhood experiences, feelings and decisions. It is the energy source, and the source of natural emotions and behaviour. There are three basic kinds of Child behaviours–spontaneous, natural responses (*Free Child*); responses which are determined by social pressures and norms (*Adapted Child*); and intuitive, problem-solving behaviour (*Little Professor*).

The *Parent ego state* is a recording of others' attitudes, feelings and ways of behaving. It is the source of positive and negative value-judgements, of permissions and prohibitions. There are three main functions of the Parent–the active giving of care and support (*Nurturing Parent*); the caring use of prohibition to protect and sustain (*Critical or Controlling Parent*) and the provision of limits and standards for guidance and judgement (*Standard-Setting Parent*). Examination and reassessment of Parent data are necessary from time to time in order to update the data and check for validity in current circumstances.

This evaluation and selection on a criterion of 'appropriateness to the here-and-now situation' are the function of the *Adult ego state*. The Adult is characterized by rational cognitive processing. It is this part of a person that can process information and events in an objective way, can estimate probabilities and likely outcomes, and make decisions based both on present and past

> experience. The Adult can use both internal and external data, can assess the relevance of data, can hypothesize, and can model reality in abstract thinking.
> A diagramatic way of showing this approach to personality structure is given in figure 9.2. A good general account of transactional analysis can be found in the book by Thomas Harris, *I'm OK You're OK*, Pan, London, 1973.

degree of these characteristics would not seem appropriate.

It is a fundamental assumption within transactional analysis that, for an individual to be operating at his or her most effective level, all three ego states should be well developed and readily available. This does seem, broadly, to be the case with successful top managers. They all showed a very well-developed *Standard-Setting* and *Critical/Controlling Parent*. We obtained little evidence of *Nurturing Parent*, which raises the question whether managers would be even more successful if they were more nurturing. According to the textbooks, this is an important aspect of management, which would be shown in such activities as the development of subordinates. It is, of course, possible to be personally successful without nurturing subordinates, but the long-term interests of the organization would be better served if managers paid more attention to this aspect of their work. This is a common observation from those involved professionally in management development. To be fair, some MDs did place emphasis on the development of their staff, and it may be that by not asking the right questions we missed this aspect of their behaviour in relation to others.

It is clear that all the chief executives we interviewed had a very powerful *Adult*. It is probably impossible to reach such a position without it. In the Child, there was strong evidence of well-developed *Free Child* and *Little Professor*. As already noted compliant and rebellious Child were not strongly in evidence, but, since all these MDs were socially very skilled, they must be capable of moving into compliance when necessary. Indeed, they were very polite to us, which is a

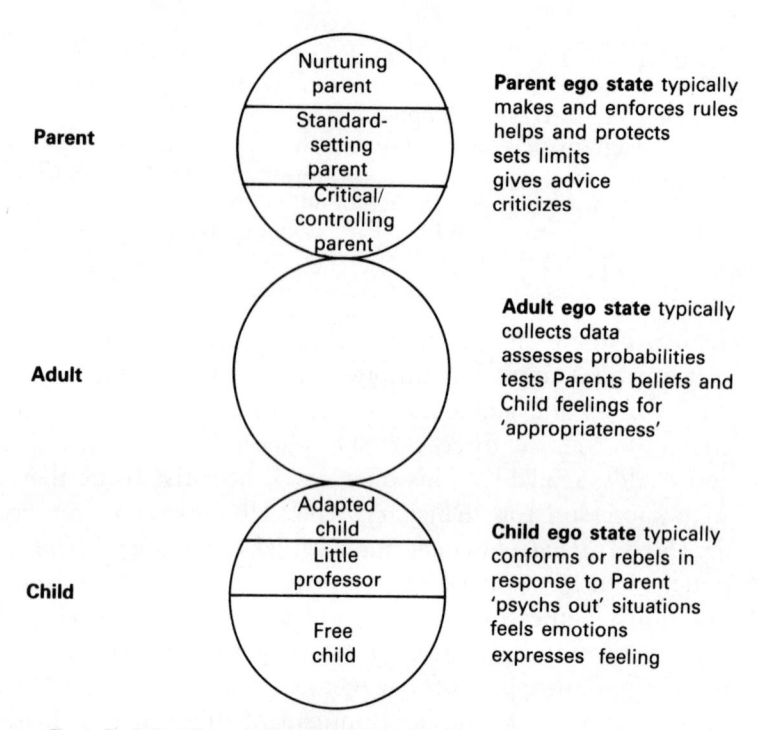

```
                    Nurturing
                    parent              Parent ego state typically
                   Standard-            makes and enforces rules
        Parent     setting              helps and protects
                   parent                sets limits
                   Critical/             gives advice
                   controlling           criticizes
                   parent


                                        Adult ego state typically
                                        collects data
        Adult                           assesses probabilities
                                        tests Parents beliefs and
                                        Child feelings for
                                        'appropriateness'


                   Adapted
                   child                Child ego state typically
                   Little               conforms or rebels in
        Child      professor            response to Parent
                                        'psychs out' situations
                   Free                 feels emotions
                   child                expresses feeling
```

FIGURE 9.2 The transactional-analysis approach to personality structure

manifestation of Compliant Child. Skill at interacting with others depends not only on the ego states which the individual has available, but on his or her ability to call on the appropriate level as occasion demands. To be totally effective, a top manager must not only develop all ego states, but must become adept at moving between them in a manner appropriate to the interaction concerned.

The Development of the Successful Managerial Personality

As with all psychoanalytic theories, it is assumed within transactional analysis that one of the main determinants of adult personality is early childhood experience. This can, of course, be modified by later experience. In the case of successful top managers (and others), two important developmental influences are education and work experience.

Early childhood There is quite strong evidence from this study and others that there are in the early childhood of successful top managers a variety of events which have the effect of throwing the individual on to his own resources very early in life, forcing him to take responsibility for himself and possibly others (e.g. siblings). These events are often associated with separation from the parents, either through death or being sent away from home for some reason. Other important influences are parental attitudes, particularly in relation to achievement and work.

Education Obviously, school and further education must contribute to some extent to the individual's development, but we found it difficult in this study to discern any clearly identifiable trends. There is a tendency for those with public school and Oxbridge backgrounds to be in the larger 'blue chip' organizations, and those with grammar school and professional training to be in smaller, more local companies. However, the school that one goes to is largely determined by parental influence and social background, so this may simply be a further manifestation of early experience. The main influence of school is probably in the development of logical abilities (the *Adult*) and social skills. Several MDs did say that they first began to recognize and develop 'leadership' and 'influence' skills at school. There is no evidence that any one type of school is better than another in this respect. It seems to be very much determined by individual teachers and the opportunities they create. For the current generation of successful top managers, formal management education appears to be largely irrelevant.

Career experience Along with early childhood, the other area of experience which does seem to be vitally important is what happens early in the individual's career. To reach the top, one must have a wide variety of experience and must avoid narrow specialization. Most MDs in the study had experienced quite high levels of responsibility at a very young age, and had been confronted with 'make or break' opportunities to which they had responded with confidence and even enthusiasm. What is particularly important is that they were successful in dealing with these opportunities. Significantly, we do not know what happens to individuals who fail in these situations. That a good 'track record' is essential is confirmed by many studies. Another important influence is whom the individual works for during his career. Many MDs recorded their debt to earlier bosses who had facilitated their development. The reciprocal of this is that the succesful manager is good at learning from his experience.

The Determinants of Managerial Success

Managerial success will be determined by three sets of factors. (1) *Management philosophy*–does the manager have the appropriate approach to managing in the context in which he or she is operating? (2) *Skills* – it is no good having the right approach if you do not have the skills to be effective. (3) *Motivation* – running a large organization takes energy and commitment, which need a high level of motivation. This motivation must also be directed to relevant goals. The needs and personal goals of a manager will be different from those of an independent professional or of an entrepreneur.

Management philosophy All the MDs in the study were very clear about their management philosophy and could articulate it without difficulty. We did wonder, at the beginning of our study, whether this would be an area of difficulty. Perhaps 'management philosophy' would turn out to be a concept that only academics were concerned with. We opened the exploration of this area with the simple question, 'Can you describe your management philosophy?' It was a question which seemed to be understood and always produced a clear response. The actual philosophy expounded was almost universally the classic 9.9 of Blake and Mouton's managerial grid, that is, a fairly equal value on both *task* and *people*, but with the emphasis on the fact that the MD's job is 'to get the task accomplished through others'. Above this, there is the general belief that the ultimate decision and responsibility does lie with the chief executive, so that in the last analysis he will if necessary make the decisions As this is recognized by his subordinates, it does lead to a subtle form of authoritarianism, which is enhanced by the CEO's general self-confidence and belief in his own abilities.

Skills The skills that chief executives reported as *essential* to their success were: (1) those concerned with analysis and problem-solving, particularly the ability to stand back from the problem and see it in all its aspects ('helicopter' quality), and also to be able to take a long-term view; (2) 'skills with people', the ability to lead a team and get the best from subordinates (this is totally consistent with their philosophy outlined above); (3) a high work rate and the abillity to work long hours.

Motivation The motivation of the successful managing director is best summarized, as we did in chpater 4, with McClelland's 'leadership motivation pattern – that is, a moderately high 'need for power' with a low 'need for affiliation' and high self-control, 'the need for power' being directed towards influencing people to achieve organizational goals (institutional power). At a more personal level their motivation is entirely 'intrinsic'; they derive a great deal of enjoyment and satisfaction from the job itself, which also provides a considerable sense of achievement and self-actualization. It is this intrinsic motivation which enables the successful MD to maintain his very high work rate and long hours.

The High Flyer: A Synthesis

The preceding analysis suggests that there are three sets of factors which are important in determining whether an individual will become a highly successful manager. These are all highly interrelated (see figure 9.3). Starting with the individual personality, a well-developed *Parent, Adult* and *Child* are essential. These will be influenced by what we have called the 'developmental experiences'. These are early childhood, education (including management education, if any) and career experience. All three of these will influence all aspects of the personality, but early childhood experience will have a particularly strong influence on the Parent value system and the Child intuition. The Adult reasoning will be most influenced by education and school experience. The three factors which actually determine managerial performance – management

DEVELOPMENTAL EXPERIENCES	THE INDIVIDUAL	DETERMINANTS OF PERFORMANCE
EARLY EXPERIENCE	PARENT	MANAGEMENT PHILOSOPHY
Develops reliance on own resources and achievement orientation	Well-integrated value system – integrity – self-reliance – achievement – initiative Control	Balanced task/ person orientation Tendency to be authoritarian
EDUCATION	ADULT	MANAGEMENT SKILLS
Including management education, if any Develops rational and social skills	Very effective analysis and problem-solving skills	Helicopter quality People skills
CAREER EXPERIENCE	CHILD	MOTIVATION
Successful response to challenge 'Make or break' opportunities	Intuition Creativity Enthusiasm Energy	Intrinsic Leadership motivation pattern

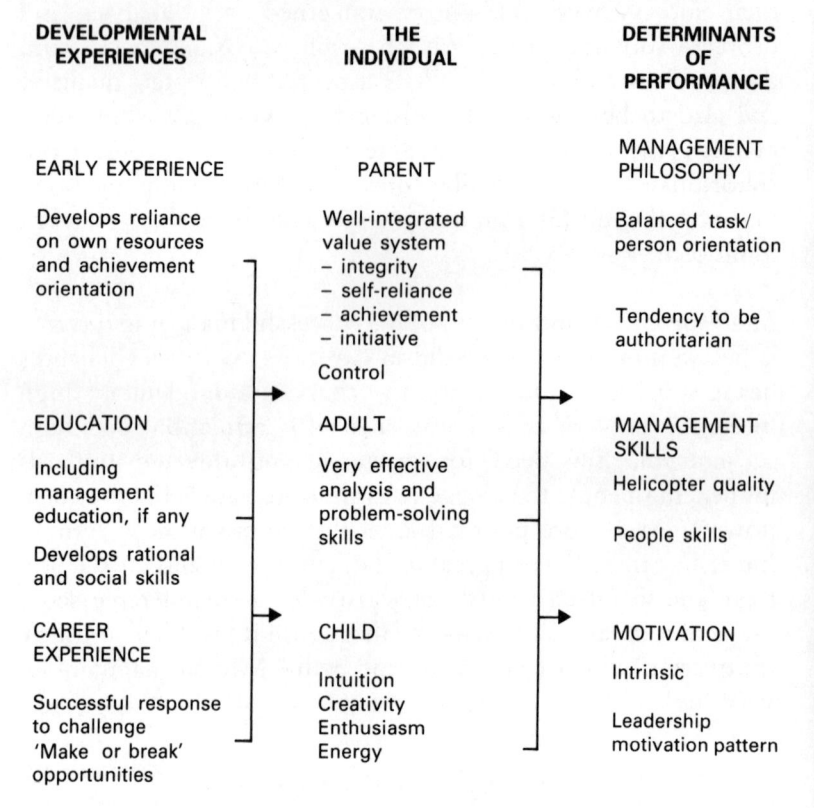

FIGURE 9.3 Factors contributing to high-flyer performance

philosophy, skills and motivation – are in turn determined by aspects of the individual. Management philosophy will be partly a product of Parent values and Adult reasoning. Skills will be determined by all three ego states. Motivation will be primarily a function of Parent values and Child needs.

SOME IMPLICATIONS

Some quite important issues are raised by this study. These have implications for both developing high flyers and selecting the individuals most likely to reach the top of organizations.

Developing High Flyers

Many organizations in the UK (mainly government and quasi-official bodies) are currently emphasizing the importance of developing managers for the future. Unfortunately, much of this activity is concerned with developing and providing 'traditional' training, ranging from short courses to MBA programmes, where the emphasis is on cognitive learning and the aquisition of information. While this activity is undoubtedly useful, it will not of itself develop high flyers. Successful top managers see their primary development coming from the 'real life' experience of being given challenging and extending assignments early in their careers. If organizations wish to develop high flyers for the future, they must be offering such opportunities to younger managers in the present, even though this will involve some risks.

An alternative and safer, but possibly less effective, option is the 'action learning' approach of providing challenging and 'real consultancy' assignments in unfamiliar industries and functions. This also has the effect of widening the individual's knowledge and ability to cope in complex and changing environments and has the advantage, in well-run schemes, of providing access to information and support from people with experience in the activities concerned. This is an asset in the early stages of an individual's development, but it is essential that at some stage he or she is given assignments which carry real value in organizational terms and for which the individual has total responsibility. These are the situations that many of the chief executives look back on as key learning opportunities. We did comment in chapter 3 that we did not know what happens to those individuals who, when given such opportunities, fail to cope with them. Perhaps more companies should develop monitoring systems and be prepared to step in with support and advice when necessary. This would be a safeguard for both the individual and the company.

There is strong evidence from this and other studies that the ability to take an overview, analyse and develop a strategy for solving problems is a vital skill for top managers. This is a skill which can be developed in a formal 'classroom' setting. Academic management programmes would probably have more impact on the 'real world' if more attention was paid to this activity, in preference to the presentation of information and abstract theory. A competent manager is quite capable of acquiring information on such issues as reading balance sheets or financial ratios when he or she needs it. Indeed, when he or she has a need for the information, it will be acquired very quickly. By 'need' we mean the requirement to apply the information in a real situation, not a need to pass an examination. The experience of the chief executives in this study is that this information can easily be acquired from short courses or from reading when it is required.

The High-Flyer Personality

Successful managers show a very wide variety of personality traits and characteristics; even those which occur most commonly, such as 'assertiveness', are not universal. This implies that there is no one ideal personality. What is important is that the manager learns how to be effective with his or her particular mix of characteristics. In some cases it may also be possible to develop missing or weaker aspects of the individual's personality. This type of learning can only occur in practical situations, either as part of life itself or in group-based training programmes aimed at developing interpersonal skills.

One quality which does seem to be universal among high flyers is *resilience* and the ability not only to cope with but also to learn from adversity. This characteristic is a function of their strong *internal locus of control*, aided by a clear *value system* and strong *self-concept*. In other words, people who reach the top are clear about *who they are* and *what they believe in*. This aspect of personality is strongly influenced by early experience and so probably has to be considered as a quality required at the selection stage, rather than as something which can be trained by the organization. Even so, some development can possibly be offered through the medium of such activities as 'outward bound' programmes, which certainly aid in the development of the capacity to overcome adversity, and do often force individuals to confront their assumptions about themselves and their values. Sensitive and skilled *mentoring* can also aid this process.

Having spent many hours listening to a range of successful people who were currently chief executives of flourishing companies, we are left with the strong impression that the most important element in their development was *real-life experience*. The role of management-development specialists should be as advisers to organizations on how to ensure that junior managers obtain this experience at appropriate times in their careers, and as support to individuals who are making development decisions. There is also a role for more formal 'academic' management programmes, whose function should be to provide basic and fundamental skills, preferably at the point in an individual's career when these skills are actually needed; and also to develop conceptual and theoretical skills which are fundamental to understanding and making sense of the world, and are thus essential for effective decision-making.

It is perfectly true that chief executives, like many other successful people, are a function of their early childhood and life experiences, or, as Milton suggests, 'The childhood shows the man, as morning shows the day.' But it is also a reality that many of the individuals we interviewed and talked to had the important quality of being able to 'get things done', regardless of circumstances or in spite of them. This quality was eloquently expressed by George Bernard Shaw in *Mrs Warren's Profession*: 'People are always blaming their circumstances for what they are. I don't believe in circumstances. The people who get on in this world are the people who get up and look for the circumstances they want, and if they can't find them, make them.' This seems to be the essence of personal success, and of Britain's future industrial survival.

REFERENCES

CHAPTER 1 THE HIGH FLYERS: INTRODUCTION

Boyatzis, R. E., *The Competent Manager: a model for effective performance*, Wiley, New York, 1982.
Bruce, R., *Winners*, Sidgwick & Jackson, London, 1986.
Cattell, R. B., *The Scientific Analysis of Personality*, Penguin, Harmondsworth, 1965.
Cooper, C., and Hingley, P., *The Change Makers*, Harper & Row, London, 1985.
Copeman, G., *The Chief Executive and Business Growth*, Leviathan House, London, 1971.
Fleishman, E. A., *Leadership Opinion Questionnaire*, Science Research Associates, Chicago, 1969.
Goldsmith, W., and Clutterbuck, D., *The Winning Streak*, Weidenfeld & Nicolson, London, 1984.
Hennesy, E., *The Entrepreneurs*, volume 1, Scope Books, Newbury, 1980.
Hertz, L., *The Business Amazons*, André Deutsch, London, 1986.
Kennedy, C., *The Entrepreneurs*, volume 2, Scope Books, Newbury, 1980.
Kirton, M. J., *Kirton Adaptation–Innovation Inventory* (Research Edition), Hatfield Polytechnic, St Albans, 1982.
Mintzberg, H. H, *The Nature of Managerial Work*, Harper & Row, New York, 1973.
Peters, T. J., and Waterman, R. H., *In Search of Excellence*, Harper & Row, New York, 1982.
Rosenman, R. H., Friedman, M., and Strauss, R., 'CHD in the western collaborative group study', *Journal of the American Medical Association*, 195, 86–92, 1966.
Sorcher, M., *Predicting Executive Success*, Wiley, New York, 1985.
Stewart, R., *Managers and their Jobs*, Macmillan, London, 1967.

Chapter 2 Origins Childhood and Education

Channon, D., 'Leadership and corporate performance in the service industries', *Journal of Management Studies*, 10, 185–201, 1976.

Clements, R. V., *Managers: A study of their careers in industry*, Allen & Unwin, London, 1958.

Cooper, C., and Hingley, P., *The Change Makers*, Harper & Row, London, 1985.

Edwardes, M., *Back from the Brink*, Pan, London, 1983.

Freud, S., *An Outline of Psycho-analysis*, Hogarth Press, London, 1949.

Geneen, H. S., with Moscow, A., *Managing,* Grafton Books, London, 1985.

Handy, C. B., *Understanding Organisations*, Penguin, Harmondsworth, 1976.

Heller, R., 'The real way to the top' *Sunday Times*, London, 26 April 1987.

Hunt, J., *Managing People at Work*, Pan, London, 1979.

Illingworth, R. S., and Illingworth, C. M., *Lessons from Childhood*, E. and S. Livingstone, Edinburgh, 1966.

Kakabadse, A. K., and Margerison, C. J., 'The management development needs of chief executives', in V. Hammond. (ed.), *Current Research in Management*, Frances Pinter, London, 1985.

Lewis, R., and Stewart, R., *The Boss: the life and times of the British business man*, Phoenix House, London, 1958.

Margerison, C. J., 'How chief executives succeed', *Journal of European Industrial Training*, 3, 1980.

Norburn, D., *Corporate Leaders in Britain and America: a cross-national analysis*, Working Paper 85.19, Strategy and Enterprise Working Paper Series, Cranfield School of Management, Cranfield, 1985.

Norburn, D., *The Chief Executive: a breed apart*, Working Paper 85.18, Strategy and Enterprise Working Paper Series, Cranfield School of Management, Cranfield, 1986.

Norburn, D., and Birley, S., *An Empirical Test of Upper-Echelon Theory*, Working Paper 86.01, Strategy and Enterprise Working Paper Series, Cranfield School of Management, Cranfield, 1986.

Whitley, R., Thomas, A., and Marceau, J., *Masters of Business: the making of a new élite?*, Tavistock, London, 1981.

Chapter 3 Career Development

Bennis, W., and Nanus, B., *Leaders: the strategies for taking charge*, Harper & Row, New York, 1985.

References

Clements, R. V., *Managers: a study of their careers in industry*, Allen & Unwin, London, 1958.
Constable, J., and McCormick, R., *The Making of British Managers*, British Institute of Management, Corby, 1987.
Cooper, C., and Hingley, P., *The Change Makers*, Harper & Row, London, 1985.
Copeman, G., *The Chief Executive and Business Growth*, Leviathan House, London, 1971.
Darman, R. G., 'In search of pioneer spirit', *Wall Street Journal*, 20 March 1987.
Garfield, C., *Peak Performers*, Hutchinson, London, 1986.
Goldsmith, W., and Clutterbuck, D., *The Winning Streak*, Weidenfeld & Nicolson, London, 1984.
Handy, C. B., *The Making of Managers: a report on management education, training and development in the United States, West Germany, France, Japan and the UK*, National Economic Development Council, London, 1987.
Kakabadse, A. K., and Margerison, C. J., 'The management development needs of chief executives', in V. Hammond (ed.), *Current Research in Management*, Frances Pinter, London, 1985.
Lewis, R., and Stewart R., *The Boss: the life and times of the British business man*, Phoenix House, London, 1958.
Livingston, J. S., 'The myth of the well-educated manager', *Harvard Business Review*, 49, 1, 79–89, 1971.
McCall, M. W., and Lombardo, M. M., *Off the Track: why and how successful executives get derailed*, Technical Report No. 21, Centre for Creative Leadership, Greensboro, 1983.
Margerison, C. J., 'How chief executives succeed,' *Journal of European Industrial Training*, 3, 1980.
Mills, D. Q. *The New Competitors*, Wiley, New York, 1985.
Mumford, A., Robinson, G., and Stradling, D., *Developing Directors: the learning process*, Manpower Services Commission, Sheffield, 1987,
Norburn, D., and Birley, S., *An Empirical Test of Upper-Echelon Theory*, Working Paper 86.01, Strategy and Enterprise Working Paper Series, Cranfield School of Management, Cranfield, 1986.
Revans, R. W., *Action Learning*, Blonde & Briggs, London, 1980.
Rogers, C., *Freedom to Learn for the 80s*, Merrill, Columbus, 1983.
Sorcher, M., *Predicting Executive Success*, Wiley, New York, 1985.
Weinstein, A. G., and Srinivasan, V., 'Predicting managerial success of Master of Business Administration (MBA) graduates', *Journal of Applied Psychology*, 59, 2, 207–12, 1974.
Whitley R., Thomas, A., and Marceau, J., *Masters of Business: the making of a new élite?*, Tavistock, London, 1981.

Chapter 4 Work and Motivation

Cooper, C., and Hingley, P., *The Change Makers*, Harper & Row, London, 1985.
Copeman, G., *The Chief Executive and Business Growth*, Leviathan House, London, 1971.
Garfield, C., *Peak Performers*, Hutchinson, London, 1986.
Haire, M., Ghiselli, E. E., and Porter, L. W. *Managerial Thinking: an international study*, Wiley, New York, 1963.
Hall, J., and Donnell, S. M., 'Managerial achievement: the personal side of behavioral theory', *Human Relations*, 32,1, 77–101, 1979.
Hertz, L., *The Business Amazons*, André Deutsch, London, 1986.
Hertzberg, F., Mausner, B., and Snyderman, B., *The Motivation to Work*, Wiley, New York, 1959.
James, W., 'Letter to W. Lutoslawski, 6th May,, 1906', in H. James (ed.), *The Letters of William James*, Atlantic Monthly Press, Boston, 1920.
Kushel, G., *The 4%*, Sidgwick & Jackson, London, 1985.
McClelland, D. C., 'Achievement motivation can be developed', *Harvard Business Review*, Nov.–Dec. 1965.
McClelland, D. C., *Power: the inner experience*, Wiley, New York, 1975.
McClelland, D. C., and Boyatzis, R. E., 'Leadership motive pattern and long-term success in management', *Journal of Applied Psychology*, 67, 6 737–43, 1982.
Maslow, A. H., *Motivation and Personality*, Harper & Row, New York, 1954.
Mills, D. Q., *The New Competitors*, Wiley, New York, 1985.
Mumford, A., Robinson, G., and Stradling, D., *Developing Directors: the learning process*, Manpower Services Commission, Sheffield, 1987.
Norburn, D., *Corporate Leaders in Britain and America: a cross-national analysis*, Working Paper 85.19, Strategy and Enterprise Working Paper Series, Cranfield School of Management, Cranfield, 1985.

Chapter 5 Values

Clare, D. A., and Sanford, D. G., 'Mapping personal value space: a study of managers in four organisations', *Human Relations*, 32, 8, 659–66, 1979.
Cooper, C., and Hingley, P., *The Change Makers*, Harper & Row, London, 1985.

REFERENCES

England, G. W., and Lee, R., 'The relationship between managerial values and managerial success in the United States, Japan, India, and Australia', *Journal of Applied Psychology*, 59, 4, 411–19, 1974.
Goldsmith, W., and Clutterbuck, D., *The Winning Streak*, Weidenfield & Nicolson, London, 1984.
Hertz, L., *The Business Amazons*, André Deutsch, London, 1986.
Hopson, B., and Scally, M., *Lifeskills Teaching: education for self-empowerment*, McGraw-Hill, Maidenhead, 1980.
McCall, M. W., and Lombardo, M. M., *Off the Track: why and how succesful executives get derailed*, Technical Report No. 21, Center for Creative Leadership, Greensboro, 1983.
Mills, D. Q., *The New Competitors*, Wiley, New York, 1985.
Peters, T. J., and Waterman, R. H., *In Search of Excellence*, Harper & Row, New York, 1982.
Rokeach, M., *The Nature of Human Values*, The Free Press, New York, 1973.
Sorcher, M., *Predicting Executive Success*, Wiley, New York, 1985.

CHAPTER 6 MANAGERIAL SKILLS

Bennis, W., 'The artform of leadership', in S. Srivastra and associates (eds), *The Executive Mind*, Jossey-Bass, San Francisco, 1983.
Bennis, W., and Nanus, B., *Leaders: the strategies for taking charge*, Harper & Row, New York, 1985.
Close, J. M., 'Dogmatism and managerial achievement', *Journal of Applied Psychology*, 60, 3, 395–6, 1975.
Coleman, J. C., *Psychology and Effective Behaviour*, Scott Foresman, Glenview, 1969.
Copeman, G., *The Chief Executive and Business Growth*, Leviathan House, London, 1971.
Garfield, C., *Peak Performers*, Hutchinson, London, 1986.
Goldsmith, W., and Clutterbuck, D., *The Winning Streak*, Weidenfield & Nicolson, London, 1984.
Hall J., and Donnell, S. M., 'Managerial achievement: the personal side of behavioural theory', *Human Relations*, 32,1, 77–101, 1979.
Heirs, B., *The Professional Decision-Thinker: our new management priority*, Sidgwick & Jackson, London, 1986..
Lennep, D. J. van, *Adaptibility to Change*, paper presented to Unilever General Management, 1963.
McCall, M. W., and Lombardo, M. M., *Off the Track: why and how successful executives get derailed*, Technical Report No. 21, Center for Creative Leadership, Greensboro, 1983.

Mintzberg, H. H., *The Nature of Managerial Work*, Harper & Row, New York, 1973.
Muller, H., *The Search for the Qualities Essential to Advancement in a Large Industrial Group*, Carel van Bylandtlaan, The Hague, 1970.
Mumford, A., Robinson, G. and Stradling, D., *Developing Directors: the learning process*, Manpower Services Commission, Sheffield, 1987.
Stewart, R., *Managers and their Jobs*, Macmillan, London, 1967.
Watson, C., 'Leadership, management and the seven keys', *The McKinsey Quarterly*, Autumn 1983.
Zaleznik, A., 'Managers and leaders: are they different?', *Harvard Business Review*, May –June 1977.

Chapter 7 Management Philosophy

Bennis, W., and Nanus, B., *Leaders: the strategies for taking charge*, Harper & Row, New York, 1985.
Blake, R. R., and Mouton, J. S., *The Managerial Grid*, Gulf Publishing, Houston, 1964.
Cooper, C., and Hingley, P., *The Change Makers*, Harper & Row, London, 1985.
Copeman, G., *The Chief Executive and Business Growth*, Leviathan House, London, 1971.
Fleishman, E. A., *Leadership Opinion Questionnaire*,, Science Research Associates, Chicago, 1969.
Geneen, H. S., with Moscow, A., *Managing*, Grafton Books, London, 1985.
Hall, J., and Donnell, S. M. 'Managerial achievement: the personal side of behavioural theory', *Human Relations*, 32,1, 77–101, 1979.
McGregor, D., *The Human Side of Enterprise*, McGraw-Hill, New York, 1969.
Mant, A., *Leaders We Deserve*, Martin Robertson, Oxford, 1983.
Mills, D. Q., *The New Competitors*, Wiley, New York, 1985.
Miyajima, R., and Cox, C., *A Transactional Analysis of Manager–Subordinate Relationships in both British and Japanese Cultures*, Occasional Paper No. 8701, Department of Management Sciences, UMIST, Manchester, 1987.

Chapter 8 Personality

Bortner, R. W., 'A short rating scale as a potential measure of pattern A behaviour, *Journal of Chronic Disease*, 2, 87–91, 1969.

References

Cattell, R. B., *The Scientific Analysis of Personality*, Penguin, Harmondsworth, 1965.
Close, J. M., 'Dogmatism and managerial achievement', *Journal of Applied Psychology*, 60, 3, 395–6, 1975.
Copeman, G., *The Chief Executive and Business Growth*, Leviathan House, London, 1971.
Eysenck, H. J., and Eysenck, H. B. J., *The Eysenck Personality Inventory*, University of London Press, London, 1963.
Garfield, C., *Peak Performers*, Hutchinson, London, 1986.
Kirton, M. J., *Management Initiative*, Acton Society Trust, London, 1961.
Kirton, M. J., *Kirton Adaptation–Innovation Inventory* (research edition), Hatfield Polytechnic, St Albans, 1982.
Kirton, M. J., 'Adaptors and innovators–why new initiatives get blocked', *Long Range Planning*, 17, 2, 137–143, 1984.
McCall, M. W., and Lombardo, M. M., *Off the Track: why and how successful executives get derailed*, Technical Report No. 21, Center for Creative Leadership, Greensboro, 1983.
Rosenman, R. H., Friedman, M., and Strauss, R., 'CHD in the Western collaborative group study', *Journal of the American Medical Association*, 195, 86–92, 1966.
Spillane, R., *Achieving Peak Performance: a psychology of success in the organisation*, Harper & Row, Sydney, 1985.

Chapter 9 The Anatomy of Managerial Success

Berne, E., *Transactional Analysis in Psychotherapy*, Grove Press, New York, 1961.
Blake, R. R., and Mouton, J. S., *The Managerial Grid*, Gulf Publishing, Houston, 1964.
McClelland, D. C., and Boyatzis, R. E., 'Leadership motive pattern and long-term success in management', *Journal of Applied Psychology*, 67,6, 737–43, 1982.

INDEX

action learning 44, 173
achievement
  motivation for 54–5, 63
  orientation towards 157–8
adaptation–innovation inventory 5, 140–1
adaptors 5, 136–41
Adult ego state 165

career
  development of 23–46
  and early responsibility 29–30, 40–1; and experience 28–9; and luck 31–2; and risk 30–1, 142
  patterns 25–7
  planning 33–4
  progression 27–8
Catell's sixteen personality factors (16PF) 130–8
chief executive
  characteristics of successful 156–62
  education of 18–20
  personality of 133–55
  qualifications of 19–20
  skills of 89–101
    in analysis and problem-solving 89–94; to achieve high work rate 97; key areas

of 98–101; in leadership 95–6; in learning from failure 96; with people 94–5; in risk-taking 96–7
  work pattern of 51–3
Child ego state 165
childhood 11–17
  detachment in 13–14
  deprivation in 8
  events in 11–16
  experiences in 16–17, 22
  influences in 8–10
  parental influence in 14–15
  separation in 12–13
communication 122
conformity 141
consideration 118
consultative style 116–18
creative discontent 58

decision-making 93
determination 157
development of high flyers 173–4
dogmatism 153

education of chief executive 18–20
efficiency 141
ego state 165
ego strength 154
espoused theory 111

INDEX

extrovert 128-9

family, importance of 65-8
fast track trap 40

helicopter quality 101
high achievers 48
high flyers 156-76
  characteristics of 156-63
  development of 173-4
  personality of 164-8, 174-6
hygiene-motivator theory 50

innovation 162
innovators 5, 136-41
instrumental values 79-80
internal locus of control 151, 158
intrinsic motivation 159
introvert 128-9

Japanese management philosophy 124

leaders and learning 43
leadership 95-6
  characteristics of 103-4
  definition of 102
  motivation pattern of 62
  opinion questionnaire on (LOQ) 5, 111, 118-19
learning
  from adversity 157
  from experience 36-9
  from failure 96
locus of control 151, 158

management
  development in 23-4, 34-6, 43-5
  and managerial success 43-5; from real life experience 44
  philosophy of 106-25
  of openness and rationality 119-24

rationality of approach in 89-90, 122
managers as leaders 101-3
manager's
  activities 87-8
  characteristics 103
  grid 107, 109-10, 120
  roles 87-8
  skills 86-101
  social origins 10-11
  success 170-1
  value system 79-84
  values 72-9
    achievement 75-6; being yourself 78; honesty 74; independence 76-7; initiative 77-8; integrity 79, 81-2; people and relationships 73-4; perfection 79; self-reliance
managing director *see* chief executive
Maslow's need hierarchy 48-9
mentors 37-8
motivation 47-50
  achievement as 54-5, 62-3, 75-6
  of high achievers 48
  intrinsic 159
  and need hierarchy 47, 48-9
  patterns of 53-9
  success as 61-4
motivators 54-63
  achievement 54-5, 62-3, 75-6
  affiliation 63
  ambition 55-6
  interest and involvement 53-4
  poverty, escape from 15-16
  power and influence 59, 63
  working with people 57-8

Need for Achievement (N Ach) 63
Need for Affiliation (N Aff) 63
Need for Power (N Pow) 63

Index

objectives, clarity of 158–9
observation 132
open management 115–16
organizational learning 100
originality 141

Parent ego state 165
parental influence 14–15
peak performers 99, 153
person orientation 111–13, 114–15
personality 126–8
  of chief executives 133–55
  definition of 127
  measurement of 128–32
    tests and questionnaires for 132
  traits 128–31
philosophy of management *see* management, philosophy of
policy-making skills 91
power 59
  need for 63
pragmatic approach 159–60
problem solving 89–93

qualifications of chief executives 19–20

risk, management of 158
risk-taking 96–7
rule/group conformity 141

self-assessment, 132
self-confidence 153–4
self-empowered person 83
16PF 130–8

social origins of managers 10–11
socio-motivational drives 63
sole-mentor syndrome 43
strength through adversity 17
structural analysis 164–7
structure 118
successful managerial personality 16
  development of 168–70

task orientation 113–15
terminal values 79–80
theory
  in use 111
  X 107–8, 119–20
  Y 107–8, 119–20
transactional analysis 164–8
type A/B
  behaviour 5, 142–3
    of chief executives 147–50
    and coronary heart disease 141
    questionnaire 145–50
type A/B
  personality 141–4, 162
values 70–85
  and decision-making 72–84
  of chief executives 72–84
value system 70–2
  of managers 79–84

wife and family, importance of 65–8
work ethic 71–2
work pattern of chief executives 51–3